MANCHESTER PUBLIC LIBRARIES

This book must be returned on or before the latest date entered below. Failure to do so will involve the payment of a fine. The loan may be extended only if the book is returned to the library to be redated and if it is not required by another reader.

FAILURE TO RETURN A BOOK AFTER DUE WARNING
MAY INVOLVE A PENALTY NOT EXCEEDING £100

G331   M/c 835

D1610875

COME SHINING THROUGH

COME SHINING THROUGH

Dilys Gater

CHIVERS
THORNDIKE

This Large Print book is published by BBC Audiobooks Ltd, Bath, England and by Thorndike Press®, Waterville, Maine, USA.

Published in 2005 in the U.K. by arrangement with Capall Bann Publishing.

Published in 2005 in the U.S. by arrangement with Capall Bann Publishing.

U.K. Hardcover ISBN 1–4056–3346–8 (Chivers Large Print)
U.S. Softcover   ISBN 0–7862–7574–X (Buckinghams)

The text of this Large Print edition is unabridged.
Other aspects of the book may vary from the original edition.

Set in 16 pt. New Times Roman.

Printed in Great Britain on acid-free paper.

British Library Cataloguing in Publication Data available

Library of Congress Cataloging-in-Publication Data

Gater, Dilys.
    Come shining through / by Dilys Gater.
       p.   cm.
    ISBN 0–7862–7574–X (lg. print : sc : alk. paper)
    1. Gater, Dilys. 2. Psychics—Biography. 3. Large type books.
    I. Title.
    BF1027.G37A3 2005
    133.8'092—dc22   2005002612

Dedication

To

Sara Keane

Marisa McGreevy

James Gross

and

Jim Diamond

to thank them for having faith in my books

And to Mark Campbell

whose photographs captured

someone to have faith in

Note

Rough Rhymes of a Padre by 'Woodbine Willie' (G. A. Studdert-Kennedy, M.C., C.F.) was published in 1918 by Hodder & Stoughton Ltd.

Contents

Introduction

To travel hopefully is a better thing than to arrive
                                    Robert Louis Stevenson

In my work as a psychic I find that most of the difficulties people bring to me, their problems and pain, arise from the fact that either they never seem to get anywhere or else they seem to have arrived at somewhere where they do not want to be. They may also feel they are trapped in the wrong place and cannot leave it.

The journey of life is fraught with other, more subtle perils and we can despair at times because we do not actually seem to be progressing at all. However hard we try we appear to be 'going nowhere'. But often we are driven in ways we do not recognise. In some cases our journey may take us backwards as well, as or even instead of, going the way we expect and want to go, along the path ahead. We may find ourselves travelling upwards or downwards or going bewilderingly sideways. We may make our voyages of discovery by learning to transcend the confines of the body—particularly if the pain of physical existence seems too difficult to bear. Or we may be required to trek deep into the wilderness of uncharted territory

1

within ourselves.

All folk myth and legend is concerned with journeys, voyages and discovery. These ancient tales recount in symbolic form the struggle of the individual, the ordinary person like ourselves, to find the answers to the great questions of existence that make life so difficult. Why must we love only to have to part? Why must we suffer or have to watch others suffer in helplessness? What is the purpose of it all? Is there any purpose, or is life just one long obstacle course, a huge cosmic joke at our expense?

Angry, bitter thoughts can plague us during our dark moments. In times of great sadness and loss we can find ourselves overcome, believing there is no sense to be made of anything in the world, wanting to give up because the way is too hard. We can feel like children wandering with no hand to hold, no light to guide us.

Most people consult a psychic such as myself because they feel they have somehow lost their way. Whether they are successful in the eyes of the world or not, however wealthy or apparently blessed with everything, they may be inwardly desperate. They may be at a crossroads, not knowing which way to go. They may have found themselves in tough terrain and doubt whether they can survive. They may be longing to return to paths they have abandoned, but cannot find the road back. They may be sunk in a pit and cannot climb out, or wandering in dangerous country where there are dragons.

The heroes of myth and legend were not gods. They were exactly like us, ordinary individuals who through their own determination and personal courage discovered unsuspected strength within themselves that enabled them to perform heroic deeds. Like us they had to venture into strange kingdoms on their quest for answers, for their promised treasures, for the ultimate reward, their Holy Grail. They too had to brave dragons and confront giants, monsters and the powers of the dark. And they returned from their travels worn and scarred, but wiser and nobler from their experiences. Often though, they did not find the answers they were looking for—or else discovered that those answers only posed further questions they could not answer.

The journey of life does not actually lead us anywhere. The whole concept of arrival is an illusion, since an arrival—or even a departure—is only a further stage along the way. Ends turn into new beginnings, partings become meetings with new forms of existence.

If you have lost your way or feel life has somehow passed you by and left you to fend for yourself, if you are abandoned and alone, hurt or anxious, in shock or sorrow, I hope you will find something here for you. Things may not even be as bad as that. You may just need reassurance that you are not trudging along pointlessly, a few words of comfort and encouragement so that you too can face up and, like the heroes of old, emerge from the dark and 'come shining through'.

Chapter 1

A Part to Play

'Call forth your actors'
William Shakespeare
A Midsummer Night's Dream

Most of us have little difficulty in being aware of who we are, but we can have problems when we come to consider *what* we are. Surely, we might imagine, it is the same thing? But a very large proportion of the people who consult me are there simply because they have never managed to identify themselves, never managed to discover what their true role in life is intended to be.

They assure me they have no real problem, there is nothing wrong they can put their finger on. Yet in spite of all the blessings they are so thankful for and count every day, still something seems to be missing though they cannot explain what it is. They are confused, unhappy, vaguely disappointed and unsatisfied —but they have no idea why.

Some sort of shake-up, a personal spiritual awakening, can happen to anyone at any time though more often than not it occurs in mid-life, particularly to women. It can come most unexpectedly, often as a great shock. It is generally nothing you might have planned—or indeed as in my own case, ever envisaged in your wildest dreams.

I had spent years pursuing a career as a professional author and never seriously contemplated being able—or even wanting—to do anything else, when my fate caught up with me. Overnight almost, I was working out in the public domain as a psychic and healer. I had made no conscious 'change of direction' or planned a career move. Yet when the unbelievable happened I could not help but recognise its innate truth, and its rightness for me.

Even more important was that I was able to see how everything in my past had been a preparation, a learning process if you like, for what was to come. Yes, I still write books but now they are mostly about and certainly reflect the psychic work I do. My vocation as a 'wise woman' and all that it involves is my real calling. I have in fact been 'second sighted' and a potential 'wise woman' all my life but was not aware of my destiny and not able to appreciate my abilities during my early years.

It is this lack of awareness that can cause so much confusion and unhappiness in many people's lives. In my particular case the failure to recognise my psychic gifts resulted in actual disaster—breakdowns and physical illness. One of the unwritten rules of universal law states that when all is well, then all will go well. It is when we are not going the way we are meant to go that our lives become fraught with problems, emotional entanglements and barriers we cannot seem to overcome. Recognition of our true role generally brings with it the kind of effortless simplicity that makes everything seem so obvious we wonder how on earth we could have missed the point for so long.

One of the questions I am most often asked is: 'How did you become a psychic?'—or indeed, how does anyone become a psychic? It is true that some people are born into families of sensitives, inheriting the gifts from a mother or grandmother and learning to handle their abilities from a young age. But there are just as many who have started their life in quite a different role in some other sphere of activity and may even have been very successful—one medium I met, for instance, had previously been a top fashion designer.

As I did, such people experience some kind of traumatic awakening, a blinding light of self-revelation that turns their whole life upside down and opens up a completely unexpected way of existence. They may not ask for such a destiny and sometimes are not at all sure whether they want it since any vocation involves a great deal of personal sacrifice, complete dedication and a letting go of the ego, the sense of self (especially of self-importance). Such experiences can be painful and frightening as well as thrillingly exhilarating.

But though of course we are not all intended to take up new roles as mediums or psychic counsellors, nevertheless the kind of revelations which are likely to transform our lives are always of a spiritual nature, and as such may be difficult to accept. If we see a vision, witness the hand of fate extended, are shown the path of destiny—particularly if this is something we would never have imagined or expected—the immediate reaction of any ordinary person is to do a mental double-take and say rather blankly: 'Who, me?'

We do not expect things like that to happen to the likes of us. We do not anticipate or know how to cope with miracles, angelic revelations, information that opens up worlds and possibilities we did not really believe existed. It is only natural to assume that such things are strictly reserved for others, for people marked out in some way, those who can live their lives by a higher code and more elevated standards than we ordinary folk can manage.

Sometimes I have 'seen' a powerful spiritual destiny ahead for some hesitant, doubtful sitter. When I describe it, the response is a rather dazed: 'But how can that be for me? I am not special, not in that way.'

Those who find it difficult to believe in their innate eminence of spirit—however this manifests itself—need to be gently reminded that it is actually rather high-handed of them to insist on emphasising their own unworthiness. This attitude reflects an inverted arrogance just as deeply rooted in self as the more usual lofty and superior attitude to the rest of the world.

'Well, I am not a saint,' Charlotte, a psychic friend protested loudly the other day when I mentioned that sainthood was a very difficult path to tread.

'How do you know you are not?' I asked. 'If it is your destiny to be a saint, and that is what God and fate has in store for you, don't you think you are being smug and self-important to keep on arguing you are "too humble"? It smacks of Dickens' Uriah Heep, always that smarmy " 'umble servant". I'm sure all the really great people throughout history would have told you quite sincerely that they weren't particularly special either—but nobody, even a saint, is born with a halo, you know.'

She looked surprised but said thoughtfully, 'Yes, I suppose you're right.'

'It is not up to you to decide what you are,' I told her. 'None of us is in a position to do that. But what we can do is make a conscious decision to accept whatever it turns out to be and do our very best to be it well.'

I am not especially widely travelled, but one of the most beautiful and sacred places I have ever visited is Delphi, in Greece. I was there for less than twenty-four hours, as a package-tourist on a week's conducted coach tour round the classical sites—details of which I used later as a background for a romantic thriller called *From Greece with Love*. Like most visitors to this ancient shrine though, I have never forgotten the impression of shining glory glimpsed there.

The light in Greece is special in itself, its sunlight white rather than golden and Delphi, situated high above the sea, seems to hang suspended in timelessness. Below its narrow streets a tide of silvery olive trees sweeps down the hillside in constant delicate movement. Above, lifting the eyes to the burning arch of the sky, tower the immense rocky outcrops called 'the Shining Ones' and beyond them the heights of Parnassus. Somewhere between earth and sky, in an atmosphere still vibrating with awful mystery, the old gods walk amid the pillars and ruins of the shrine where in ancient times, petitioners came to seek wisdom.

The priestess at Delphi—known as 'the Pythia'—gave answers from the god that she was granted 'in the smoke'. As she sat entranced and the vapours of the ground itself mingled with the scents of burning incense, the god to whom the shrine was dedicated—in later times and most famously, this was Apollo—spoke through her, answering the questions brought by pilgrims. In the language of prophecy and divination (which we will be examining later in the book) the future was revealed and enlightenment bestowed.

But apart from what they might have been told privately in the chamber where the Pythia sat, visitors to the shrine found wise words of instruction written within the temple for all to read. The most famous, as well as perhaps the simplest, was the brief and cryptic admonition to 'Know Thyself'.

People concerned with their life path or their future consult a psychic asking for information about what is likely to happen, what they should do. But in fact the first step along the way forward is to follow the advice given to all at Delphi and to look within. We need to spend time getting to know ourselves, discovering who and what we are as truthfully as possible. It is only when we have identified and accepted our own particular role as a traveller along the highway, that we will begin to appreciate exactly where we have come from and where we are now, as well as how we came to be here. With this enlightenment it becomes possible to identify where we are heading and in which direction we truly want to go.

Our upbringing in the western world dictates that most of us assume we are being selfish, vain and/or arrogant if we spend time thinking about and dwelling on, the subject of ourselves. We are inclined to apologise if we do it, and so one of the great benefits of a sitting with someone like me is that the person having the consultation is actually encouraged to talk about his or her feelings, thoughts and opinions frankly and openly in a relaxed atmosphere.

Any counsellor, psychic or not, is well aware of the therapeutic value of being able to do this. Whatever impression we would like to give, for whatever reason, it is a strain to continue making efforts to keep our real selves hidden. The presentation of the picture we want the world to believe is the 'real us' can be extremely difficult to maintain. Stress, tension—even actual physical illness—can result. So how wonderful to feel free and safe enough just to be exactly what we are, to say exactly what we think and feel and believe for once, without fear of judgement or recrimination! Even if we are our own harshest critics (and many of us are), the true self will not go away. We cannot escape our own eyes and what we see there when we look at ourselves, however much we wish it could be different.

I cannot speak for other counsellors or psychics but I am sure they would agree with me that the kind of work we do brings us into contact with a great deal that is socially and/or morally regarded as unacceptable in a 'decent' community. I regularly encounter every kind of sin and vice from greed and envy to fornication, adultery and sexual excess and indulgence in many varied guises. I speak to victims of rape, abuse and cruelty, and to those who are (whether unwittingly or not) perpetrating cruelty on others. On several occasions I have 'seen' that the person sitting with me had actually committed murder.

I encourage people to talk to me about themselves but this is not for my own benefit, since I can 'see' into their souls without assistance. Neither is it, as cynics maintain, so that I can pump them for details I will be able to claim I saw or knew by other means. 'Second sight' is intuitively aware of the basic truth about everything it encounters and nearly everyone I speak to is only able to give me their own side of the story—a half-truth at best which is highly biased.

So I encourage sitters to talk not in order for them to reveal themselves to me, but so that they can reveal what they really are—their true selves—to themselves. Whatever reaction I might have to them as human beings, whether I approve of them personally—even whether I actually like them or not—is irrelevant. My role as a counsellor and consultant is concerned not just with helping sitters to see themselves more clearly but with assisting them to be able to accept what they see in a positive and constructive way, without being crippled by guilt, shame or fear.

The fact that I am a psychic goes deeper. My role here is to reflect what I can 'see' of their souls in the same way that a mirror reflects what is visible of their physical appearance. Because I am more aware of their inner being rather than the defensive mask they present to the world, I find that when I speak to people I generally speak to their potential selves rather than to their disguise. This can make for very stimulating and challenging consultations that reveal unexpected virtues, strengths and depths within themselves to my sitters. They depart, I hope, comforted and encouraged that the efforts they have made in the past have not been unnoticed or pointless; empowered to try even harder in the awareness that they can succeed at making their lives different in the future.

Sometimes though, the basic truths will stretch people further than they are prepared to go. During sessions conducted 'soul to soul' as it were, even the most unlikely sitters often surprise me with the width and scope of their personal vision, their intuitive wisdom and honesty. They will admit to awareness of obstacles blocking their progress that they do not recognise or want to own up to in their worldly persona. They will even discuss what action they might take to overcome such obstacles to a higher way of life with remarkable frankness and humility. And yet, after the consultation is over they invariably slip back into being almost a complete stranger to the one I have just 'seen' sitting opposite to me.

Even their actual appearance can sometimes seem to change. I might have been talking to a woman I perceive as young, hopeful, smoothly fresh-skinned and with a diffident, lovely smile. The face becomes the authoritative sophisticated made-up mask of the cosmopolitan head of a business in her fifties as we say goodbye.

Or it may be the opposite way about. Recently a young man had a sitting with me at a Psychic Fair and someone else commented afterwards that he had seemed very adolescent and unsure of himself. But I had been aware only of the immense stature of the soul within his thin frame. He had advanced towards me dwarfed in an over-large raincoat, nervously enquiring if I was free and I had seen not the youthful, bespectacled English college student but a mature man of amazing wisdom and power. I saw too that with him and overshadowing him there was someone Jewish, in late middle age. He had been a very eminent professor or doctor (of the mind rather than the body) who I 'saw' had died in a concentration camp during the Second World War. He would be working with and through this young man in the future when he was ready for his destiny, and as he left I felt it was I who should be thanking my sitter for the privilege of having met him, not the other way round.

When people try to visualise 'The Future' they generally regard it as something concrete that they have to aim at like a hoopla prize in the funfair. If we want to be sure of a bright future

16

we must struggle to get our ring over the prize with our name on it. Then bingo! We are guaranteed to be happy ever after!

But what if we should miss this glittering prize: what if we do not choose 'the right road' or go 'the right way'? The prospect seems too awful to contemplate and many people are quite unable to take pleasure in today because of their ever-present anxiety about what might go wrong tomorrow. Some even point out to me in complete seriousness that they simply must have detailed and accurate information about their future 'because otherwise I can't possibly make any long-term plans.'

They seem to imagine that I (or indeed, psychics in general) have been given a kind of personal hot-line into the future. Our 'sight' is assumed to bestow the ability not only to reel off what lies ahead as though daily schedules are contained in a sort of tourist brochure, but to conduct negotiations with the fate doing the organising so that a satisfactory outcome can be guaranteed. Such sitters are not so much interested in hearing about what is likely to happen, as explaining about the things that will be very inconvenient for them if they do occur. Then they sit with hopeful faces waiting for a response, as though they expect me to say brightly:

'Right, I'll have a word with Head Office about that. I'm sure we can get it sorted for you.'

We are so used to the customer always being right and our wants as consumers being met by those eager for our custom that (especially since they genuinely regard their requests as perfectly reasonable), people can be disconcerted to be informed they will have to take the future on trust. There is no way anyone, whether psychic or not, can do a deal, make a bargain or negotiate with God, whoever or whatever he perceives God to be.

It would of course make things easier if we knew exactly what tomorrow and all the tomorrows after that would bring; if we could start to organise on a long-term basis, prepare for calamity, muster our resources, stockpile against disaster. Even if we know things are going to be difficult we can buckle down, grit our teeth, steel ourselves and prepare for a long haul.

In many ways it is easy to see why humanity is so preoccupied with doom and gloom and generally fears the worst. We are accustomed to struggling for survival since this is the natural state of all living things. In fact the circumstances of everyday existence in a physical world conspire from the moment we are born to make it extremely unlikely that we will survive for any length of time at all. The prospect of our actually managing to escape accident, illness, violence and all the things that could cut off our breathing or stop our hearts beating, crush, maim or mangle our physical bodies for forty—sixty—eighty or ninety years is something no bookie would give you odds on.

The fact that we have reached this present moment—now—is an incredible achievement in itself and when we appreciate this we can see that taking the future on trust actually does make sense, even though more 'rational' brains would have us believe otherwise. As newly born babies we took the future on trust because we did not know how to do otherwise and somehow we have all managed to get here more or less in one piece. It is truly miraculous—and the chances are that our future will be just as splendid and amazing if only we will allow it to be.

When we discover how and what we are intended to be, the question of what we are to do will take care of itself. Psychic vision is generally rather vague anyway so far as hair-splitting details are concerned.

I encourage people worrying over decisions to imagine that they are looking back in ten, in twenty years from now. I ask them whether they think all their sleepless nights and anxious weighing up of the 'what ifs' and 'if onlys' will have made any serious difference to the eventual outcome of their life's grand plan. Viewed this way, nearly everything that potentially looms in a terrifyingly large and unsurmountable way can be immediately reduced, placed in a better perspective. The effect is of great burdens being eased from our shoulders. We are able to lift our heads, to breathe, to mentally flex our muscles and loosen up—and consequently far more likely to cope with any problems that do crop up and take them in our stride.

The intricacies of living apparently so vitally important, minutiae that pull us down and preoccupy our every waking thought, can seem at the time such life or death affairs. What if I fail my exam? What if I fail my interview? What if this love affair is only an infatuation? The more choices modern life allows us—about possible careers, relationships, retirement prospects, all allowing our individual personalities the freedom to express themselves —the more we can become bogged down as we try to untangle the knots that surround every decision in order to make the 'right one'. But there is no 'right' decision, there is no one sure way, just as there is no one sure prize as we stand with our hoopla ring in our hand preparing to take aim into the future.

If we miss the 'right one'—even if we keep missing all the 'right ones'—it makes no difference. The fact that we tried, that we made the effort and did our best is what counts. We will not find ourselves thrown out into the dark, abandoned forever having lost our only chance. We all make mistakes, we all fall and so long as we pick ourselves up and try again, sooner or later we will make an attempt that will succeed.

Details such as exams, tests, whether we meet the standards and criteria of the people around us, of our social class, of what we see in the media, of what we think we should aspire to—all these fade into insignificance when we consider the wider perspectives of our existence. What matters is whether we as individuals face up to our lives with courage and fortitude, teach ourselves to learn from our experiences however painful or bitter, and manage to grow in personal stature and maturity. These are the true measures of living with which 'the sight' is concerned. There are far broader perspectives, far wider vistas, far subtler values than the milestones by which we normally measure our lives—or with which we normally try to map out our future.

Certain things in our lives are, however, fated

to happen. Some believers regard these as settlement of our karmic debts—if they are wonderful blessings we did not expect we have earned them in a past existence; if they are difficult roads along which we have to tread then we need to atone for wrongs committed in our previous lives.

Most people are far more aware of the difficulties. But instead of losing heart in the face of what seem like great obstacles in our way, we should welcome them as challenges to be overcome. They teach us necessary lessons in our spiritual progress and whether we want to learn these lessons or not we will find that often, until we are prepared to face up to them and deal with them effectively, they will continue to confront us.

The card in the tarot pack known as 'Judgement' relates to this kind of problem or situation. When it appears it indicates fate and destiny at work, a passing through some preordained gate, a trial or ordeal that cannot be avoided. It is true that every individual has freedom of choice. We can choose whether or not we will walk the path that has been marked for us and learn the lessons we have been set— but what we cannot do is dictate our own life path and set our own lessons for ourselves.

When we are shown the path of destiny we

must tread every step even though the prospect ahead may not be what we would have preferred if we had had any say in the matter. We must take a positive attitude, tell ourselves it will all work out for the best even though we do not want to endure or accept the situation. For however many times we may try—or may have tried in the past—to go sideways, rush the other way without looking or pretend we did not see that particular road we will find we keep being brought inexorably back to it.

If we examine our lives we will see how similar patterns recur time and again. When we seem to have escaped from one disaster we will voluntarily plunge ourselves into exactly the same situation. And though we are always advising others to learn from their mistakes most of us remain blissfully ignorant of how to do this ourselves. When the 'Judgement' card appears it reminds us that we are here for a reason. We all have a task to carry out in this life and our purpose, our individual destiny, is to learn to acquire the strength and wisdom necessary to confront and resolve the particular problem each of us has been set.

Destiny is not necessarily something spectacular or earth-shaking that will mean we are remembered by posterity or have our names in history books. It is the genuinely modest, humble soul that regards itself as far too flawed to fulfil a heroic role which is probably already treading its destined path and achieving immensities. Such souls might well be unaware of their achievements—and sometimes those around them are unaware too—but what they have accomplished is clearly visible to 'the sight'. Often just as visible is the lack of true depth and spiritual immaturity in smug, superior types who claim—usually loudly and publicly—to be following a path of high destiny and enlightenment.

The destiny each of us has to fulfil is concerned, as it was for those heroes of ancient tales and folk myths, with spiritual progress, increasing awareness and the acquiring of wisdom. Many aspiring and novice psychics or even those who just want to 'live a good life' or 'be' clamour eagerly for instruction about the best way to go about achieving this desirable state.

They are willing to do anything, they say. They are only too eager to undertake any task they might be set, however arduous or impossible. They promise that if necessary they will meditate for hours, read volumes of books, give up everything from designer clothes and luxuries, alcohol, cigarettes and fleshly pleasures, to their actual homes and families.

Yet once again we can see that the real quest does not involve *doing*. If we follow the advice given at Delphi all that is necessary is to look within and discover how to *be*. The most difficult lesson in living wisely and heroically so that we can fulfil our destinies does not come from applying our will to making ourselves perform arduous physical tasks. There is no need to undertake a long and demanding journey, volunteer for back-breaking labour or force ourselves to go without life's pleasures so that we can congratulate ourselves we are in the process being 'spiritual' and 'good'.

All we need to do is simply to let go of our selfish wants and wishes and our ideas about what we consider would be best for us, and accept the destiny we have been assigned, the role we are required to play, in faith and trust.

Rather surprisingly it is the most spiritually advanced souls who have to struggle hardest. The greater the gift of awareness, the greater our awareness of our own failing. This is why we 'wrestle with our angels' and fight against our higher destinies though in our hearts, we know we are denying what we are most desperately seeking and longing for. Even psychic and sensitive people are as human as everyone else in this respect.

All self-help systems and manuals for success and happiness insist somewhere that it is imperative each person learns to love himself or herself before he can begin to achieve his aim. And loving yourself means first and foremost loving what you actually are, not trying to love a self you would like to be or a self that does not really exist if you are honest. As to achievement, each individual carries the seeds of his future within himself and when you are prepared to truly know and accept yourself, you will not only know what your future is to be, you will become that future.

Our deepest fear is that we are inadequate.
Our deepest fear is that we are powerful beyond measure.
It is our light, not our darkness that most frightens us.

Nelson Mandela

Chapter 2

The Way Back

The past is a foreign country; they do things differently there.
L P Hartley *The Go-Between*

The past holds the key to both today and tomorrow. It is the ghosts of our past, the trailing threads of all our unresolved anxieties, emotions and yearnings that cause most of the problems we are likely to find confronting us in the present. These in their turn can prevent us from being able to view the future with hopeful optimism, not in themselves but because they seem to have become so snarled and entangled they are now impossible to unravel.

If only, if only we could go back into the past and re-live it, do it over again. How often we sigh and shake our heads as we contemplate the mistakes a headstrong younger generation is making, the problems they are laying up for themselves. We know we made the same mistakes in the past and now, too late, with the benefit of hindsight we can see only too clearly where we went wrong.

One of my favourite aphorisms uses the language of the theatre to warn us that *Life is not a rehearsal*—it is more in the nature, perhaps, of an audition. You only get one chance to impress, to make your mark and put yourself across.

There is no training for life, no preparation, you are out there in the spotlight without a script and there is no prompter! You improvise as you go, you have to act on your feet, you don't know any of the actors who appear on the stage with you or what part they are supposed to be playing—and you haven't even been told the plot! What makes it even worse is that you know when the curtain comes down that will be that. This is a single live performance. There will be no repeats, no videos, no film. A few 'still' photographs in an album might well be all that is left of this, your starring role.

Time is an amazing and wonderful thing. It does not actually exist as such and before the concept of chronology presented us with the idea of a linear existence—lives that progress forward along a kind of conveyor belt so that we move from past to present to future—awareness of life was far more flexible. The prospect of being able to see into the future or even to journey back to the past would have been something primitive people would have found entirely acceptable.

The characters in those ancient myths about gods and heroes wandered in and out of time and space, into kingdoms and realms that had no physical actuality. And of course it is possible to glimpse this kind of altered awareness of existence today. You will be familiar with it if you are any sort of a creative artist, if you write poetry, paint, listen to great music or concentrate hard on meditation. You may lose yourself in it altogether if you take hallucinogenic drugs or try to follow the practices of a shaman, unless you know exactly what you are doing.

We exist on many levels. The writer E.M. Forster commented in his book *Aspects of the Novel* that: 'Daily life, whatever it may be really, is practically composed of two lives— the life in time and the life by values.' Yet however intense our experience and though we exist in this world chronologically our situation can sometimes seem to be static, since as human beings we are not able to remove ourselves physically from a present we do not like. Trapped and bogged down by build-ups from the past, we may feel despairingly that not only will we never manage to move forward, we will never be able to move in any direction at all.

29

However determined we might be to live a better life or make our future more positive, we cannot wipe the past out and start off again with the equivalent of a clean slate. We cannot make a sudden transition from present to future, to leap into the day after tomorrow or the middle of next week and simply jettison all the baggage we carry with us. Those clinging inadequacies, guilts, hurts and resentments, dreads and fears cannot just be ignored or abandoned, however much we would like to leave them behind. We remain—and on one level will always remain—in exactly the same place, in the present moment where the past has gone and the future never comes yet we have to be prepared to carry the responsibility for them.

It may well be this realisation that triggers off the personal spiritual crisis which as we have seen, probably occurs in mid-life. However difficult existence might be, most people continue to plod along hopefully, believing vaguely that somehow things will sort themselves out. They will meet the 'right' partner who will save them, a prince on his white horse who will sweep them off their feet and 'take them away from it all'. They will find a job that brings fulfilment as well as success and riches, make a home in some special house in just the right neighbourhood where they can live happy ever after.

There must be an answer somewhere. We have all felt like this. But as the years go by and no answer is forthcoming, disillusion begins to creep in followed by despair and sometimes bitterness. Surely this is not what life is all about? We begin to question what we have been taught, what we have been told. We start trying to probe deeper, to try to find the answers for ourselves—and so the spiritual journey begins.

Because the roots of most present problems and pain lie in our past, in childhood or even babyhood, we need to return to the past if we are to deal with them. This journey has to be made symbolically or mentally since it is obviously impossible to return physically. But in order to heal our wounds and help us to see the way ahead more clearly, return we must— even psychiatry, the 'science of the mind', works on this principle. Before we can let the past go and be free to move on, we need to face the traumas we repressed or tried to ignore because they were too painful for us to cope with at the time they actually happened.

Hypnotherapy is one method used to facilitate a return to our early years so that we can resolve this kind of unfinished business. In trance we can even re-experience birth or return to existence in the womb. Medical science now concedes that such a thing is possible. But what about returning to, or recalling, the lives we might have lived before this one?

The question of reincarnation, whether we have lived or will live other lives on earth in addition to the life we are experiencing at this moment, is one some people find difficult to take seriously even though it forms a part of the belief of many religions. But during the years I have worked as a psychic I have encountered a surprisingly large number of people who can remember their earlier existence without the aid of trance and whether they want to believe in reincarnation or not.

Young children are particularly psychically gifted and are able to relate easily to recollection of lives they might have lived in some other time or body. It is our upbringing and social conditioning that blots out such awareness or sends it underground as we grow. We learn that we will probably be considered 'different' or even mad if we admit to any recollections of this kind and most people keep their personal psychic experience— including the ability to remember past lives before this one—strictly to themselves.

I mentioned a case in my book *Understanding Past Lives* where an eight-year-old boy remembered being burned to death in an airship when it caught fire. I do not usually work with children but I have met many adults—perfectly 'ordinary' people generally—who have told me during consultations or sometimes just when talking socially, that they are aware of having lived a previous life: in some cases, lives. Often they have not discussed their awareness even with their closest family.

One of the reasons for their reticence is that it is almost impossible to convey the ordinary, natural quality of an experience of this kind to anyone who has not shared the same or a similar awareness. Recollecting a previous existence is not the eerily spine-chilling procedure that popular horror and fantasy literature would have us believe. It is not particularly significant in any religious way and has nothing to do with 'whether I accept the principles of reincarnation or not'. To those who experience past life recall, it is very little different to having recollections of childhood in this life and just as seemingly 'normal'.

I have never come across anyone who regarded their recollections as in any way 'spooky' or alien to their current experience.

They may well have been defensive or apologetic when telling me the details but it was the fact that they could not account for what they were saying or explain it away in scientific terms that bothered them, rather than the experience itself. They were afraid of being told they were imagining things, inventing stories or being dismissed as foolish or crazy.

But such recollections seem so mundane and natural, absorbed into the pattern of each person's *now*, that they may even feel irritated at having to elaborate or enter into discussions about them. We do not feel obliged to weigh up, question and discuss the random memories we might have of running along the sands when we were a child or visiting another country when we were a teenager.

Regression to past lives is usually carried out under hypnosis. The practitioner puts the subject into various levels of trance and the results can be examined in the same light as medical case notes: they need have no connection with the world of psychics and mystics or religious belief.

But any consideration of whether we have lived before cannot help but raise questions of a spiritual nature, often questions formal religion does not seem to answer for us. And since the psychic is recognised as working with and living an other-worldly sort of existence, the interested enquirer is often more likely to consult a psychic than, say, a theorist, a professor of religious studies or a minister or doctor.

It is often possible for psychics to 'see' past lives with their inner vision, sometimes spontaneously or else while reading the cards, working with the crystal or using some other tool for focusing 'the sight'. I have had results with both these methods but more often as I have explained in my previous books, I work by 'linking in' to previous existence for sitters simply by concentrating my mental energies while 'holding' them in my mind. A clear image comes through, sometimes a very detailed one which I can then relay to the person concerned.

I have never tried to account for how this is achieved, though the results have often been surprising and amazing. It is to me just one more aspect of the gift of 'second sight', being able to use my inner or 'third' eye in order to 'see true'. Various authorities have explained the process as the psychic ability to make contact with or 'tune in' to what are called the Akashic records, a cosmic pool of consciousness where everything that has ever happened (and perhaps everything that is ever going to happen as well) is stored.

At the beginning of my psychic career I was inclined to be open-minded about concepts like this. I was very chary of talking in 'alternative' jargon and felt rather self-conscious if I referred to 'vibrations', 'auras' or similar terms. But over the years my experience increased and I also read widely, studying the various dimensions of the world in which I was now living and working, its principles and laws as well as its literature. As an ordinary, reasonably rational and intelligent human being I had found my own 'second sightedness' very difficult to adjust to and accept let alone speak of with authority to others, but I discovered that most spiritual concepts are actually backed up by recognised and respected theories—sometimes even by scientific fact.

The idea of the Akashic records, for instance, as a timeless, limitless fount of all information that can be 'read' if one is able to connect with them, is not just a kooky 'alternative' theory. It is recognised in many cultures and referred to by other names—the most popularly known, perhaps, being the all-embracing Jungian concept of the 'Collective Unconscious'.

Kate consulted me in some desperation because she suffered from a crippling 'phobia'.

'I cannot bear to look at buttons', she said. 'On clothes, anywhere, they just make me terrified. I get really sick, ill. I have to wear things that have no buttons on them, and my husband has to do all the ironing. Shirts, blouses with buttons—I can't deal with them. I just cannot do it. And I'm afraid of seeing buttons when I go out. You can imagine how it makes life difficult.'

None of the therapy she had been given had helped to explain her fear or alleviate her phobic reactions. She asked whether I would conduct a past life regression session to see if anything helpful emerged. Since she lived some distance away it had to be done by phone but when I 'linked in' to her past life as we began the session, an immediate picture came through.

'I can see you as a young girl, perhaps fourteen, about the time of King John.' (Late 12th Century). 'You lived somewhere in England in a very heavily wooded area, forest really, and you are walking along a path through the trees beside a stream or small river. It is quite early morning. You are dressed in your best because it is a holiday, a country fair I think, or some other day of celebration. You are wearing a long gown with a tightly-fitting bodice and have very long hair, in a braid down your back, bound with ribbons. You are very proud of all this finery and looking forward to showing it off.'

There had been a water mill beside the stream and for some reason I did not know but which seemed to be concerned with a message she had to deliver before she set off to join her friends elsewhere, the girl had entered the mill. I described to Kate what had happened next.

'You were laughing, displaying your dress and ribbons to the people inside the mill who were working. You were very close to the millstones, huge round stones that ground the corn into flour. You were moving quickly, talking and showing off like any adolescent looking forward to a day out and somehow your long braid of hair got tangled up—perhaps between the stones, but it might have been into whatever machinery was working them. You could not pull free. It was over before anyone could save you—you were caught by the hair and your head was pulled in and crushed between the stones.'

Kate had suffered a sudden and horrible death which had, I thought, traumatised her so that her spirit remained trapped in that instant of time. Even more clearly, I saw the reason for her unusual phobia.

'As your spirit left the body at the moment of your death, it rose up. You were able to look down on yourself lying there—and what you actually saw, what held the attention of your spirit in its last moments of awareness, were the millstones, huge pale circles that got smaller and smaller as you rose higher out of your body. You perceived them simply as round circles standing out against the dimness, the shape most buttons are. I think that is what causes your fear. Not the buttons themselves but what they represent to you—the powerful force that took your life away.' Kate neither refuted nor accepted what I saw.

'What can I do about it?' she asked bluntly.

I pointed out that confronting one's trauma generally eased the fear and reduced it to manageable terms.

'Well, how can I confront what you saw? Having my head crushed in?' she persisted.

'I think you need to go out and find your real fear, your real underlying problem. The buttons are only symptoms, symbols,' I told her. 'You need to go on some sort of a journey—a journey of self-discovery, if you like. It is always easy to say "I am suffering too much to make any effort, I will just sit back

39

and let other people do it". I'm not trying to minimise your suffering, Kate, but you need to examine your feelings honestly. Do you really want to be cured and be free of this thing that separates you from everyone else, or would you rather hold onto it and feel it gives you a reason why you have been excused from facing up, as other people have to?'

She replied curtly that of course, naturally, she wanted to be cured, so I suggested that she tried to find somewhere in England where there was a water mill still working and made a trip to visit it, even if she had to travel a long distance.

'And then what?' she asked.

'I think if you have got that far you will find the answer when you get there,' I said.

She made no promise to do so and I never heard what the outcome was. But her case is particularly illustrative of complications that can emerge—often very subtly and in a less dramatic manner—where death is involved. The death may be one we may have experienced at some time in the past or the one that lies ahead of us, the death that will mark the ending of our current life-span. The subject of death—the crossing of the bridge between our world of the physical and the world of spirit—is examined in a further chapter.

Exploration of the existence we might have known in the past can make itself relevant to the life we are living in the present in the most unexpected ways. Often we are not aware of the problems that need to be resolved—and as the spool of our lives continues to unravel, new problems can occur.

When Rowena visited me it was not for a past life regression as such, but for a Reiki healing session. She was not exactly ill but was certainly suffering from tension and stress and was trying very hard to make the break from a difficult and destructive relationship. Like many people she had back trouble, and she particularly complained of an irritating skin complaint that so far doctors had not been able to diagnose or alleviate.

For a Reiki treatment the patient lies relaxed on a treatment couch while the healer gently places his or her hands at certain points, working slowly down the body. There is no massage or manipulation, the healer works within the energy field that surrounds all living matter, unblocking and clearing the centres of natural energy so that the flow is unimpaired. The body is then free to function easily and naturally, without any part of it being out of balance. This treatment is very soothing, as well as enabling the body to begin to clear itself of manifestations of stress and imbalance that usually take the form of general aches, pains and tiredness. In Rowena's case I assumed that the unidentifiable skin rash was probably also symptomatic of her stressed state of mind.

Reiki is not just a method of promoting physical healing and well-being. As with all holistic treatment it works on all levels—spiritual, emotional and mental as well as physical. A Reiki Master is extremely spiritually aware and as I was working, looking down at her relaxed figure, I found I was 'seeing' her in an earlier life (or rather, as with Kate, in an earlier death). Instead of the slim, attractive woman lying quietly with her eyes closed and her black hair spread round her head, dressed in jeans and sweater, I was 'seeing' the remains of an entombed body lying in a very confined space—I thought within a wall. The flesh had shrivelled over a long period of time on the bones leaving nothing around the skeleton but flakes of ancient, crumbling dust.

As I worked within the energy field I found myself clearing the debris of years—possibly centuries—away from Rowena's still form and when all was cleared and cleansed, I mentally placed the images of flowers and candles in her tiny 'tomb' and said prayers for that long-dead soul. The session left her, I hoped, not only healed and relaxed in this life but at peace in the previous one.

I told her what I had done, adding that I thought the past death had occurred at some time when she had been a priest or holy man during a time of persecution. This previous self had been walled up alive or else had become trapped while hiding in a 'priest's hole' and had died there, remaining unshriven and unburied.

Even before I began my explanation Rowena informed me that she had been aware of a great sense of increasing lightness, as though some burden was being lifted from her. She added: 'I have always been afraid of being buried alive. This makes sense to me now.'

I told her I thought it was the flaky, dusty, powdery remains clogging the atmosphere around her 'dead' self that had been irritating her skin, and that I had cleared them away. Whatever the reason, she reported the next time I saw her that the rash had almost gone.

Many patients who come to me for Reiki healing report that they experience a widening of their mental horizons during treatment.

They cannot easily explain what happens since they are not used to such awareness. They may say it was a vision or an image, something like a hallucination. In fact the Reiki Master works throughout on this level of awareness and in company with his or her 'Reiki guides', beings recognised and revered as the means of opening up other channels of natural balance and harmony.

Problems of all kinds from past lives appear and can be dealt with, often as in Rowena's case unknown burdens can be removed to relieve the sufferer. When I was doing a Reiki session for a woman who was a recovering anorexic, for instance, I found I seemed to be clearing away some kind of thick smothering dark clouds—possibly of fog, smoke or pollution—that surrounded her upper body and were dragging her down. But one can sometimes find too-pat explanations that are far too simplistic for the depths and complexity of the nature of healing. The most important thing about such sessions and what they bring to light about past lives is that though a healing session can have an almost miraculous effect, it is always the personal responsibility of patients to continue to work at their own treatment and effect a cure for themselves.

Awareness of our past lives does not always reveal secrets we did not know. Knowledge of past existence can provide us instead with a reaffirmation of our sense of true self, that self which might well have been in danger of being swamped or otherwise pushed out of existence in the tumult of living in the present. Even if we do not, or cannot overtly play a great role publicly in this life we need always to have a personal awareness of our own unique potential and destiny.

'I was a medicine man, a Sioux, I lived early in the 18th century,' said Sandra, a blond secretary, quietly and with no sense of false modesty. 'I was greatly revered, very wise.'

'I remember my whole life when I was Rebecca, the woman who was closest to Jesus,' a psychic healer told me. An ordinary middle-aged Englishwoman she had recorded tapes of herself singing 'Rebecca's' songs in a language she did not know and was able to give details of all aspects of everyday life in Biblical times.

Sixty-year-old Tom had begun to trust me enough after several consultations to reveal that he clearly recollected a previous existence as someone of royal blood.

'I was a prince and I died very young in that

life. I was drowned. I was on the White Ship and it sank,' he said, explaining that he had made efforts to identify his previous self, researching painstakingly through English history. He discovered that in 1120AD, William 'the Aetheling', son of Henry II and heir to the throne, was recorded in contemporary documents as having been on board 'the White Ship' with his entourage when it sank in a terrible storm. The teenaged prince, the hope of England, was lost with all on board, his death leading to the civil wars that tore the country apart during the reign of Stephen.

The importance of past life awareness need not necessarily be in simply revealing that we have lived as another person. Subtleties of what is revealed may highlight aspects of ourselves we have not fully understood or been able to accept in the present. Often regression sessions can provide new and unsuspected angles that turn the familiarity of our current existence on its head and clarify the cause of on-going problems.

I first became aware of this on the very first occasion I was regressed under hypnosis. When asked to describe who and where I was, I found myself to be a gentleman in middle age at the time of the English Civil Wars. I was sitting at a table in a small panelled room with some other men, holding a meeting to discuss the latest news about the political situation and the threat of imminent civil disturbance and plan what action they should take locally. These were men of some influence, landowners and gentry, concerned with the protection of their families, homes, villages and neighbourhood. They were also arguing over their own individual political loyalties.

What I found fascinating was that the regression was so limited and incoherent. The man I had been in the past seemed unable to contribute anything to the discussion. He was shocked—perhaps even physically ill— confused and slow to react. I was aware of a fog of bewildered hopelessness within in his mind, an actual withdrawal from the problems around him, great tiredness and defeatism. A mature man perhaps in his mid-fifties (though I sensed he was considered 'old' then—and felt old too), a country gentleman of some standing in the community, he was at that moment completely out of his depth.

What amazed me was how different his mind and his whole personality and attitude had been from my mind in this life. The thought processes were far slower and he questioned things less. And yet somehow I understood everything about that mind, it was not strange to me. In the same way I do not query my own sense of awareness of self now, I did not do it then. I 'knew' that self too—I had occupied that mind, I had been that man.

At the same time I was able to evaluate on my present level, with my present brain. I was aware of historical facts he knew nothing about. England had been on the brink of civil war yet I could not tell which side he and the other men had been on—I did not think they knew themselves. Their conversation was inarticulate, uninformed and they were wearing plain shirts and coats in dark colours that did not suggest either 'Roundhead' or 'Cavalier' to me.

I found it fascinating to be living and experiencing moments when the history of which I was intellectually aware in my current existence had yet to be created. These men were indecisive, arguing between each other, the younger ones boasting and shouting, the distant political scene and all that it implied very much in the background of life. All that seemed to matter to them was what was going to happen in their own immediate environment—to their own land and property, homes and families and the way of life they knew.

This seemingly unspectacular regression revealed a great deal to me about myself. The elderly man had been unable to cope, he had felt as though events were beyond his control and I was able to relate his bewilderment and sense of helplessness to my own feelings at that time. Often we do not know exactly what our feelings in this life are. We think we know, but our lack of self-awareness can be so great that however realistic and down-to-earth we might appear, we could actually be occupying a fantasy world. And it is extremely difficult for us to relinquish the delusions and defenses we have so carefully erected to try and protect ourselves from hurt within that world.

Many people are unable to follow their destiny and fulfil the heroic role intended for them because they cannot abandon the comforting importance of a role they have created for themselves—generally a role that reinforces their sense of being necessary, of being needed. Ingrid's was a typical case. Charismatic, dynamic, she existed as the forceful hub around which her family and friends revolved. Even though she had survived a painful divorce and suffered a combination of health problems that verged dangerously near to potentially life-threatening, she insisted on 'being there' twenty-four hours a day for everyone else and did voluntary work as well as her full-time job.

When she consulted me she was tired and tearful, on the verge of breaking down. I could see that in common with many such people she was a perfectionist, inwardly desperately insecure, her lack of confidence leaving her wide open and vulnerable. I pointed out that she needed to rest, to relax and take things easier for a while. But even as she tried to control her tears she insisted: 'I have to keep going, I can't afford to take a break and think of myself. My parents are elderly—Dad is not well—they need me there for them more than ever now. And then there is Louise, my daughter. She lives with me, but of course she will get married some time and settle down and until I know she is secure and happy I have to be there for her too. I know what the world is like, what men are like, I have knocked around and I want to make sure she is not hurt.'

I tried to provide the reassurance she so badly needed that her efforts were valued and appreciated, that her contribution (which she perceived as the only measure of her personal worth) really counted. But I suggested that maybe she actually owed it to those she felt were dependent on her to give herself some time 'off duty' and not push herself so hard. After all, if she broke down she would not have any choice over whether she was able to 'be there' for everyone else.

It was not her responsibility to carry the rest of the world. In fact surely it was rather arrogant to assume that she was intended to do so? Her parents might need to feel they were respected as individuals still able to make decisions and cope, in however limited a way. And her daughter Louise was twenty-four, no child but a mature woman herself who had to be allowed to face up to the challenges of the world in her own way in order to gain her own experience of life.

But Ingrid would not even consider the thought that anyone could manage without her. She declared bravely that though she was sure I meant it well, she could not possibly think of herself when there were others to put first. No, she would soldier on somehow.

Until we can see that we do not need to act out every part in the play ourselves and accept the role intended for us in gratitude and humility, we will always be afraid of failing. No-one is indispensable and the world will continue to turn whether we are there or not but what a disagreeable notion this is to our egos, what a slap in the face for our childish certainty of self-importance.

I anticipated that Ingrid's daughter probably suffered from extreme frustration but when she had a sitting with me I discovered she was far more spiritually mature than her mother. She smiled when I suggested she might feel a need to rebel, to break out and 'do her own thing'.

'I'm happy as I am, just being myself. I don't need to rebel, I have nothing to prove—to myself or anyone else. And so far as Mum's need to be there for me is concerned, well, I love her. I don't need her to take me on board but if it's something she has to do, I have no problem in letting her do it.'

I have mentioned in all my books that everyone intuitively possesses self-awareness. We all know the truth deep down but often will stubbornly not admit it and it is just as futile to indulge in past life regressions as it is to look for help from any other source if we will not accept the evidence that is revealed and learn the lessons the past has to teach us.

Like Ingrid, many of us find it dismaying to have to let go our conviction that we are necessary and that our absence would leave a yawning gap that could never be filled. Even psychics find it hard to let go the ego. Don, a medium I had worked with for several years, was particularly low one day and when I offered to do a reading for him I 'saw' that apart from material worries, the main cause of his trouble was that he had apparently lost his faith. He was working not with the higher power of Spirit but from reserves of nervous energy generated by himself—something workers in spiritual and psychic fields can be driven to do if they have lost the spark. They continue to function somehow by drawing on past experience, too arrogant to admit they have gone wrong, but their refusal to humble themselves and seek the path they have lost only alienates them further from the true source of their inspiration.

When I told Don what I saw, he candidly admitted it. We can all suffer from crises of faith and I sympathised with his inward doubts and sense of isolation—but I was surprised and disappointed to hear he was not prepared to wait until he had regained his spiritual path before continuing his work. It would have meant greatly reducing his income for a while, and since he was a very 'fashionable' psychic medium this was considerable. He had no intention of giving up any part of the luxurious lifestyle he enjoyed.

I never did an in-depth reading for him again and our paths diverged soon afterwards so I never knew how—or even whether—he found his faith again.

The card called 'The Lovers' is generally assumed by people who have no knowledge of the tarot to refer to an imminent love affair. But in fact, in the commentary that the tarot provides on life's spiritual journey, 'The Lovers' signifies a choice, a splitting of the ways. Sooner or later we all have to face those two paths and choose whether we will continue along the way of the physical and material or whether we will strive to follow the way of the spirit, a higher calling. If we have not been able to make the choice in our previous existence we are given the opportunity to make it in this life—often as I have mentioned previously, over and over again.

Laurie, a young woman trapped in a destructive relationship she had endured for years, told me quite clearly when she sat down for her session: 'I am at a crossroads and there are two ways I could go.' She informed me of the choices she could make and was very self-aware. 'I have been here so many times before, you see, but I have not been able to actually take any steps forward. This time I must. I don't think I can stand any more. But making the decision is so hard, isn't it?'

This is true, yet when considered rationally, it does not actually make sense. I pointed out to Laurie that whichever way she chose to go, she could hardly be worse off than she was with the status quo. Any kind of positive step at all could only improve matters. Yet still she hesitated, and though she had come to ask for help to make her decision, she left with her mind as undecided as it had been when she came in.

The trouble is not in seeing the way forward or even knowing what to do about it or which way to go. It is not even—as in Laurie's case— being unwilling to make a change or lacking courage or strength.

'I am such a weak person,' Laurie said, but I indicated her cards, assuring her: 'You are far from weak. You are amazingly strong or you would not have survived what you have endured already. But you are applying all your energy to doing the equivalent of dragging a heavy ball and chain around with you. If you decided to let it go, you would still be strong— yet you cannot see that one can be strong and happy, only that one has to be strong and miserable. You could use your energies to enjoy life rather than fight against it.'

She pleaded: 'Tell me which way to go, then.'

'No,' I told her. 'This is the real crux of the matter, Laurie. I cannot make the decision for you and neither can anyone else. All the troubles in your past were caused because you were trapped in situations based on power struggles, forced either to do what you were told or to rebel against the people and circumstances controlling and manipulating you. For you to escape that situation you have to do more than just find somebody else to give you the orders. You have to realise you are responsible to yourself and must make your own decisions and stand by them. You know in your heart that I am right, but this is the really hard part—to stand on your own feet and choose for yourself.'

Whether the answer lies in a past life or in this one, it is difficult to let go the ball and chain so many of us drag round with us and take control of our destinies. The ghosts who haunt us are not only of our previous selves, they can be phantoms of distorted emotions, long-dead loyalties, unrealistic dreams and ambitions that have their place in the childhood of this life. Even the inability to let go of that childhood, our memories of that distant country where they did things differently, can trap us and hold us stagnating, frustrated and increasingly despairing that we will ever be able to move on.

Because we are so obsessed with doing we are generally completely unable to see that there is no need to do anything except be true not to our delusions, but to ourselves.

*We ask ourselves: 'Who am I to be brilliant, gorgeous, talented, fabulous?' Actually, who are you **not** to be?*

Nelson Mandela

Chapter 3

Mystery Tours

And I said to the man who stood at the gate of the year:
'Give me a light that I may tread safely into the unknown.'
And he replied: 'Go out into the darkness and put your hand into the hand of God. That shall be to you better than a light and safer than a known way.'

Minnie Louise Haskins

Do we have free will or are our lives predestined? Do we create our destiny ourselves or is everything already decided, so that we have no control over what will happen to us?

We have already seen that both these alternatives are true, and they are reflected in the ways in which seers and psychics attempt to view the future. Many methods of divination have been used since the beginning of time, some of them frankly amazing to our modern way of thinking. I once made a list of a hundred and thirty known ones, including the following which are particularly spectacular:

Alphitomancy

Divining the guilt of suspected wrongdoers from forcing them to eat wheat or barley cakes. The innocent were able to swallow the cakes, the guilty choked on them.

Anthropomancy

Reputed to have been practised by the emperor Julian the Apostate. The intestines of ritually sacrificed children were examined and interpreted.

Cephalomancy

Practised by the Lombards, who poured lighted carbon over the baked head of a goat or other animal and divined from the result.

Cromniomancy

The omens were read from observation of the skins, sprouting and general appearance of onions.

Gastromancy

Divining by interpreting the sounds made by, or appearance of the belly.

Geloscopy

The interpretation of a person's laughter.

Hippomancy
Consideration of the running of horses and their attributes. This was practised by, amongst others, the ancient Celts, who held the horse in great veneration. One of the most powerful Celtic goddesses was the horse-goddess Epona (from whose name comes our modern word 'pony').

Myomancy
Much practised by the Ancient Romans, Ancient Egyptians and in Ancient Assyria. The squeaks and squeals of rats and mice and their other activities, were observed in order to divine the future.

Tyromancy
Divining from observing the coagulation of cheese.

All forms of divination are based loosely on two main types of system. One kind is intuitive, here the 'sight' is all. The other sort—like astrology, numerology or palmistry—are more formally based on rules, workings out and calculations, though often the intuitive 'sight' is present as well and it is difficult to identify where the rules end and the intuitive vision takes over.

In the cases of prophetic dreams, awareness of imminent happenings, visions of natural disasters and in some formal readings based on weighing up of the rules of the system, what is generally considered as having been revealed to the seer is the 'future without', the actual future, what will actually happen. But more subtly, especially when the revelations are about the real nature of the person or people concerned and their likely decisions and courses of action, the seer will get a picture of the 'future within', the potential future, what will possibly—or probably—happen.

Somewhere between the actual and potential futures that lie ahead of each of us is the future we can create for ourselves. However inauspicious the circumstances from which any human being has come, however deeply influenced by heredity and upbringing—the twin strait-jackets of 'nature' and 'nurture'—we are all free to reach within ourselves to the deepest resources we possess and change what seems to be our destiny. But our sense of self-importance may well be trying to delude us even about some praiseworthy attempt to overcome it: perhaps the struggle to alter the course of our destiny was actually what we were really destined to do all along.

The road any individual will choose to take is something that can never be foretold accurately and this is what often accounts for confusion over predictions that do not appear to come true—even predictions that seem to have been quite wrong. The psychic can often see and predict events that might happen, some that will probably happen and even some that will almost certainly happen but it is impossible to see or know at any stage exactly how everything will turn out.

John A. came to see me because he seemed to be stuck in a rut—but it was his lack of self-awareness that made him his own worst enemy. He told me he had visited several psychics and seers over the years and all of them had told him he would marry. Some had even given him a specific date for the event—one said he would marry at thirty. But now, aged nearly sixty, he was still single and gloomily indignant about his lonely state.

He admitted when I questioned him, however, that he had actually spent his entire thirtieth year (and all the other dates that he had been given as possibilities for marriage) very much on his guard, grimly determined not to be 'trapped' into any kind of a relationship. I could see that in addition to a remarkably strong and determined will, he also possessed a deeply hidden, fatalistic and compliant streak that would have made him vulnerable to manipulation by a certain type of personality. Because of this I considered the seers had probably been quite accurate in their predictions: he would almost certainly have married (probably at the age of thirty and seemingly quite willingly) if he had not gone to such extreme lengths to 'protect' himself. The single-minded focusing of his energy and intent, employed to over-ride the possible, even probable future had enabled him to create his own actuality.

George was another who came to me with a tale of woe, having been assured, he claimed, that he would in later life 'live and work in the sun'. He had assumed his dreams would all be fulfilled. He would write successful best-selling books in some sunny Mediterranean villa, and had looked forward for years to giving up his everyday job as a plumber to enjoy the fruits of international fame. He was hurt and disappointed when he consulted me since retirement was almost on him and he could see no way now that he would ever achieve what he thought he had been promised—literary greatness and the money and lifestyle that went with it.

I mentioned earlier that the language of prophecy and divination can seem confusing. It is always essential to know exactly what was said, to have the exact wording of any prediction about the future. When I questioned George about the prediction that had meant such a great deal to him I discovered that the tarot card around which it had centred had in fact been the card known as 'The Sun'. And it is true that when this appears it does usually indicate a very favourable outcome. Problems will be overcome, dreams will be fulfilled and life will seem bright and good—but this need not actually mean we are presented with every item on a request list we have pushed beneath the nose of fate.

I pointed out to George that it was his own interpretation of what constituted a 'good life' which had painted that highly-coloured 'sun, sand and success' scenario. Actually, his circumstances were very comfortable indeed. He was financially secure, emotionally happy in a new relationship that had brought a sense of youth and joy back into his life and given fresh impetus to his literary aspirations. And though he had not yet managed to write a best-selling book, he was involved with both the local newsletter and magazine concerned with community arts, and had achieved celebrity status in a modest way. In the spirit, if not the letter, the prediction he complained had failed to materialise had actually been quite accurate.

When we are born our sense of self-importance and self-righteousness, our conviction that we and our wants matter more than anything else, is what enables us to survive. But as we mature spiritually we begin to become aware of needs that the ego, with its preoccupation with physical necessities and material desires, cannot provide. In our struggles to reach a higher spiritual plane we can often find ourselves going round in circles—we may know where we would like to go but are unable to take the one step that would get us there. Instead we take the route that goes all round the houses, stopping off and getting side-tracked into dead ends and dark alleys on the way.

Mark, a Canadian with a soft-voiced drawl, had a sitting with me. I could see in the cards that there was a high destiny before him, something I thought was almost Messianic. He had a very great deal to give and to do with his life—and more importantly, he also possessed the ability to realise everything his destiny demanded from him. Living and working in London as a highly-powered economist he seemed on the surface to be geared very much to the material and to money, but people who have a great spiritual destiny to fulfil are always aware of it, to whatever degree. When I told Mark what I could see he nodded, accepting it without hesitation.

'Yes, I know.'

We spent his session discussing how best he might go about achieving his incredible potential. I told him he would be guided, that Spirit would reveal what he was to do when the time came and he was ready.

'You are a truly great man,' I said, but was forced to add: 'Or you will be. You have not made any real effort yet to discipline yourself, dedicate yourself to the true purpose of your life, have you?'

He smiled rather complacently, like a small boy secure in the knowledge that he can get away with not doing his homework because he can charm the teacher. He was prepared to discuss his destined role, how he might alter the course of history, but not to seriously try taking any real step in that direction. I had a chance meeting with him in the City the next day and he spent an hour detailing get-rich-quick schemes in which he had involved himself, once again trusting to charm—and to luck—rather than any effort on his part. Since it was obvious he was not yet ready to take his destiny as seriously as his bank balance I left him feeling sorry rather than impressed.

One of the first things I needed to learn when I began to realise I had psychic abilities, was not to expect to be given answers to my questions. 'Second sight' does actually reveal all answers—but these may not necessarily be to the questions human self-importance and inquisitiveness lead us to ask. In the paradoxical way spiritual laws work though, it is the answers we are given that matter and not the questions we might have wanted to pose.

It was at least seven years before I visited a Spiritualist Church or had any real idea I might be psychically or mediumistically gifted, that I was granted my first conscious awareness of being provided with answers concerning the great truths of existence. My experience had something of the mystical revelatory quality of a so-called 'Near Death Experience', though so far as I know I was never actually clinically close to death.

At the time the occurrence happened I had reached what was possibly the lowest point in my life. I had recently suffered two bereavements, the deaths of my mother and my husband. I was on heavy medication, having been driven by years of depression alternating with manic 'highs' to twice attempting suicide. I felt there was no way forward for me. I could not face the world any more, but neither could I face trying once again to kill myself. And what was perhaps worst of all was that after suffering a bitter mental breakdown in my early twenties, I had lost all faith in the God and the religion I had been brought up with—Welsh Methodist, actually.

There seemed no place for me to turn for spiritual comfort or sanctuary. In my anguish, I consciously withdrew from the battle. I placed myself into the hands of something I had no name for and could not identify. I went through a kind of private (and very painful) psychoanalysis where I reviewed everything, my past awareness of being, my sense of reality, my values and my own self as honestly and sincerely as I could in an attempt to come to terms with my life, to find some meaning and a way forward.

At some point during the eight weeks while I was passing through the crisis, the experience I have mentioned occurred. It happened without my being aware of it, though afterwards I knew something of immense significance had taken place. And like all mystical revelations, like 'Near Death Experiences', like the blinding light encountered by St Paul on the road to Damascus, it changed my life—or at least, it changed my attitude to my life.

The dictionary defines 'mystic' as 'person who seeks by contemplation and self-surrender to obtain unity or identify with, or absorption into the Deity or the ultimate reality, or who believes in the spiritual apprehension of truths that are beyond the understanding.' Another definition is 'mysterious and awe-inspiring, spiritually allegorical or symbolic.' I had sent out a cry for help from the depths of despair to some kind of higher power. I did not know whether such a power existed, but I knew I could go no further alone. And this was my account of what happened to me, written a few years later:

At this time I experienced an awareness of existence at a much higher level, on a plane which is pure spirit, where there is no form, no time, nothing except unity with the Absolute. It was something that happened without my knowing it—and yet, it seemed as with truth, that I had always known it.

Many times I had sat in the doctor's surgery during those miserable years, sobbing my heart out and pleading that 'I want to go home.' But nobody could find out where 'home' was. I did not mean North Wales, where I had been born, nor Stoke-on-Trent, where I had lived most recently for ten years. I did not know where 'home' was myself. All I knew was that I longed with all my heart to be there again, in my own place, with my own kind, where I belonged. And from the glimpse I was given of this other level of existence, I gained a sense of immense comfort, the knowledge that this was my place, this was where I had come from, this was where I would return.

I received also a message from this glimpse of a higher existence, which I found soothed and uplifted me in the depths of my despair. It was one of many visions of the truth that I would be given later, as my spiritual development progressed. I tried to put it into words to explain it to D. (the person I was sharing a home with at that time):

'I just knew that everything is as it should be. It's all progressing in the way it was intended to go. All the suffering, all the pain in the world, has to be there—don't ask me why—but it is just something that has to be and somehow, it is all right. I don't mean we should accept suffering and cruelty and pain, but even our struggles against them are intended, meant. The result is already known.

It reminds me of the Bible—'He seeth the sparrow fall' and 'Every hair on thy head is numbered'. There is nothing too small or too great—it is all equal, all intended, all known in its entirety even before it begins.'

I did not see a blinding light nor a god-like figure, nor travel through the long tunnel that seems to form an integral part of reported 'Near Death Experience'. So far as I can recollect, my spirit seemed to pass through a veil into a great void that was more dark than light, though I had no human senses to perceive with. I seemed to see myself, my essential being, hanging in the void like a fragment of space within infinity, or a single drop that was itself and yet part of an immense ocean.

The experience was simplicity itself, all reduced to pure energy, simply existing. But the sense of reassurance, of belonging, of overwhelming love, was so great that when the vision had gone leaving just human memory—a petty, inferior copy of the original—I felt I had been given the keys to all knowledge, that for a brief instant I had understood everything.

I saw, as many others have seen and recorded in greater words than mine—Wordsworth in his *Ode on the Intimations of Immortality in Early Childhood*, for instance—that we come at our birth from the same home to which we will return, and that our human life span is just a brief struggle we must cope with as best we can. I realised too that however hard we try and however much we want to see the sense in everything, some pattern we can comprehend, we will never do this while confined by the limitations of our human brain, wonderful organ though the brain is.

After the experience I stopped asking myself the agonising questions: Why am I here? Where am I going? What is life for? What is it all about? I saw that it was not necessary for me to know nor to understand, simply to accept that though the meanings might not seem clear to me, they were there all the same and somewhere all the answers were known and understood.

Some of the ways we have to travel cannot possibly be planned or even envisaged beforehand and we cannot make any sense of them until we have actually completed that part of the journey and are able to look back. Then, in the same way we recognise that they were inevitable we can see that the acquiring of wisdom does not bring increasingly convoluted 'cleverness', but strips aside barriers we erect in order to try and protect ourselves from reality. The simple basic truths we knew and accepted without question as children are revealed once again.

After my journey into myself and into the void, I was left with a sense that I had touched incredible depths and heights. It had been the greatest effort of my life and I assumed my struggles had been necessary because the lessons I needed to learn were so difficult. But a few weeks later I had a conversation with my daughter, then in her early twenties.

After I had finished wrestling with myself, (I recorded in the journal I was keeping), I wanted to help Judi with my knowledge, hard and newly-won. But it is Judi who has helped me since, times I have been down and struggling.

If only my own mother had been able to turn to her daughter with humility, been able to admit her weakness and her daughter's strength and accept the love and support I would have been only too willing to give, how different and less traumatic my story might have been.

When, very hesitantly, I summoned up the courage to tell Judi what my book was about and what had happened to me, and I asked whether she would read it, adding: 'It might help you to understand—might explain—,' she cut me short.

'Mum,' she said firmly, 'you don't have to explain anything. I don't need to understand.'

It seems that to my daughter, things are simple. I am her Mum, no questions asked, no apologies necessary. She accepts me whether I am in fragments or whether I am whole, whether I am helping her or she is helping me. To her I am a person in my own right, just another woman with strengths and weaknesses travelling my own road through life. Judi already knows what it has taken me forty tormented years to find out, that each of us is 'the Captain of my fate, the Master of my soul'. She pointed out after talking with love and common-sense through an hour of my doubting and self-querying:

'We all have to have our own strength, Mum, not somebody else's. I'm the only person who's going to be here all the way through my life, every minute of it, through everything. And you're the only person who's going to be there all the way through yours.'

The role of someone who seriously considers and pronounces concerning the possible events of the future—a seer, diviner or prophet—is not generally appreciated because we all make casual predictions all the time. They are a part of everyday living:

'Oh yes, Brian is going to university, he's going to be a doctor'; 'Sally will be wanting to settle down and have a family in a few years'; 'That boy will go far, it's obvious' or even the more cryptic 'It won't be long before she gets her comeuppance' or 'That's one marriage that is never going to last.'

But according to the dictionaries, a prophet is not only 'one who foretells future events', he or she is also 'an inspired teacher or revealer of the Divine Will'. The true gift of prophecy based on genuine vision bestowed by the 'sight' bears no relevance to our own ideas of how we anticipate things will happen, how we think they should happen or even how we hope to make them happen.

The true gift of seership cannot be influenced by desires, biases or moral judgements. Quite often, what we see can shock us by running contrary to what we would like or even expect. And while it may certainly be said to express the Divine Will in some sort of general way it has absolutely nothing to do with formal religion, even though seers have always been inclined to attribute their visions to whichever deity they happened to believe in.

Though a psychic, a seer or diviner might be granted the ability to see the 'what' or even the 'how' of the future, he is rarely given any explanation as to the 'why'. This is not because his vision is flawed or he is not as accomplished as others who claim to know all the answers—it is because, as I have said, the working of the world of Spirit cannot be explained in terms the human brain can understand.

When we look back across the past we can clearly see the pattern created by the hand of fate and we will always find that fate has worked a far better pattern for us than any we might have been able to envisage for ourselves. But when we try to look forward we are peering into a dark void where events have yet to happen and their significance cannot be evaluated. We may think some shape or pattern looks as though it might be the working of the Divine Will, but on the other hand it might seem to make no sense at all.

It is our human arrogance (that troublesome ego again) which is responsible for our conviction that we are entitled to a satisfactory explanation for everything. If this is not forthcoming we tell ourselves we have a right to complain or dismiss what we are offered as Not Good Enough. Even people actively interested in what a psychic or diviner might have to tell them about their future feel justified in taking this attitude, though some individuals prefer to blank the whole thing out altogether.

'I don't want to know what is going to happen,' they say firmly, taking an ostrich, head-in-the-sand kind of approach. There is no reason why they should know of course, but generally they are consoling themselves that 'if I don't look, any bad things won't be there' rather than expressing a conviction that whatever the future might bring they will be able to face it and cope.

People who simply do not want to accept what the diviner can see have a habit of shifting their ground. If home truths about how their own attitude or behaviour will affect future happenings are pointed out, they assume patronising smiles as though they have let the game go far enough.

'Yes, that's all very interesting I'm sure,' they say in "more in sorrow than in anger" tones, 'but I'm sorry, I need real help in the situation I am in.'

What can be disconcerting about the prophetic vision is that it is far more likely to challenge us than reassure us of our superiority by bolstering up any cosy convictions we might hold about what we think 'right' or 'wrong'— even what we might consider satisfactory. It can transcend with its complete truth any formal moral judgements society might want to make. For the judgement the future will make—the divine and cosmic judgement that prophetic vision reveals as the attribute of the Divine Will—has nothing at all to do with the simplistic conception of others getting their comeuppance for being 'bad' or being rewarded for being 'good'. And the prophet or seer cannot be held responsible for what his vision reveals or be expected to justify it. He, like everyone else, is only human.

Most people who consult me are guiltily and shamefacedly conscious that they are not perfect. Though they have tried, they have made mistakes in the past. Though they do their best, they are not handling the present as they feel they should. Though they are determined they will try to tackle the future with wisdom and confidence and take all the right steps forward, they doubt secretly whether they will be able to achieve this praiseworthy ideal. Often they have already condemned themselves and feel themselves to be lacking in every way that counts in a world of high fliers. The future, they fear, will only reveal even more clearly the threadbare fabric of their pathetically limited personal achievement.

Other sitters have come to an awareness of the spiritual quest after some kind of previous entanglement in what is generally considered the seamier side of living though this may have been no more than an expression of the extreme behaviour characteristic of the struggle for growth. But individuals who now regard their past with shame may nevertheless feel irretrievably besmirched by it. Things they said or did, all that took place in the past however regretted or even paid for since, cannot be rubbed out so how can they transcend their mistakes and blunders and the damage they might have inflicted—however unintentionally—on others and on themselves? What kind of hope can they have as they look into the future?

To such hesitant, apologetic and fearful souls the vastness of what is revealed with the 'sight' can be as comforting as a warm hug. When we accept that we are not supposed to know all the answers—or even the questions—we realise we are in no position to make assessments or pass damning judgement either on others or on ourselves.

The apparently magical insights of psychic vision are achieved because 'the sight' reveals not just the parts we might want—or might not want—to see but the whole of what is there. And it reveals too that by being prepared to take the prospect of a whole that is greater than all its parts in trust and in faith, we can transcend the need both to know and to understand that whole.

The Great Spirit is aware of the fact that you are all very human beings and imperfect. This is why you are on earth. If you were perfect you would not be where you are now. The function of your earthly life is simply to eliminate your imperfections.

Silver Birch

Chapter 4

Secret Passages

Where'er we tread 'tis haunted, holy ground
Lord Byron *Childe Harold*

Everything about our existence has the potential for holiness, even the most mundane tasks, the most seemingly ugly, even revolting aspects of what we see around us. Spirituality does not necessarily exist only on some starry angelic level where there is nothing but sweetness and light.

However deeply we may be absorbed in trying to raise ourselves from the material and aspire to a higher plane we sometimes need to be reminded of another lesson we have been set to learn, just as vital and often just as difficult. We are actually here on Earth to live full and meaningful lives as material beings in a physical world. This is where, for the span of our lives, we belong and it is important that we remain 'grounded' and do not reject the world—for whatever reason—or try to remove ourselves from it either mentally or physically.

Life is never static. It is constantly fluctuating

and in order to keep our balance we have to make sure our feet are planted firmly on the ground even while we experience the wonderful sensation of losing our heads in the silvery clouds of spirit. We need both extremes for in fact it is the awareness of each that actually intensifies appreciation of the other.

All living things have an innate instinct to exploit to the full their physicality and the sheer sensuousness of their existence. Flowers bloom in the sun. Birds sing and build their nests. Any animal—including the human animal—joys in his own state simply of being alive.

And the world we perceive with our physical senses is a beautiful place. Sunrises and sunsets, thunder of surf on a rocky beach, the grandeur of high mountains, secret flowering of the first small buds of the Spring—these are the things that nurture our spirits as we grow and inspire us. They are intimations of the presence and beneficent order of whatever higher power rules the natural world. The need to save and preserve the planet that is our physical home can indeed be viewed as a cause worthy of passion for it is unlikely that the planet itself will arouse any desire to want to live 'out' of the physical. Even natural disasters or hardship imposed by problems of survival do not have this effect, rather they bring out the better nature of the human animal, rousing compassion, generosity and self-sacrifice.

What is at the root of most attempts to withdraw from our physical existence lies within ourselves, in the increasing sense of disgust and horror people feel when they become aware of the 'other side', the 'dark side' of human nature and the evils it can be prepared to willingly embrace. We may find the world an unacceptable place when we are forced to see its tragedies looming too clearly, its sufferings gratuitously intensified by the cruelty and destruction that feeds on human weakness, selfishness and greed.

All of us have a 'dark side', we are all capable of the deepest depravity and the spiritual path is the way we choose to tread in our sincere attempts to overcome these tendencies within ourselves. It is not easy and few thinking people have not at some time felt a desire— however fleeting—to 'opt out' mentally. Some individuals can be so appalled and distressed they try to ignore or minimise their own physical existence and the problems of living in a human body in a physical world.

Spiritual teachings can help us try to look at the essence rather than the outward show and to seek the divine spark within. But even if we can appreciate the innate beauty in the human condition and have compassion for human weakness we may find it hard to understand or accept any kind of pain and suffering as a necessary part of living particularly if we are very close to it. We may not see why we or the people we love are obliged to carry burdens of disability, grief, hurt or loss. Physical and mental pain can sometimes be so terrible that oblivion—a literal getting out of the world—can seem the only reasonable prospect.

One of the most complex and interesting cards in the tarot pack is 'The Moon'. This signifies when it appears that a time of spiritual growth is imminent. Traditionally the picture shows a mysterious gateway bathed in moonlight, on either side of which two forbidding dog-like animals seem to be howling. What lies beyond the gate is not clear, but in a pool of water in the foreground a crayfish (sometimes represented as a scorpion or a crab) is partly emerging.

Some tarot readers will tell you that this card has negative connotations and that it denotes denial and disappointment. You will not get what you want—you are, like the dogs, 'crying for the moon'. But spiritual growth is always difficult since as we have already discussed, one has to let go of egotistical wants and learn to simply accept what one is given thankfully. And spiritual growth—as this card indicates—is hardest of all when the transition from the material to the spiritual is first being attempted and commitment to the spiritual is being made.

The gateway between the two worlds is narrow and can seem terrifying since like the gateways into those mythical kingdoms and realms through which the heroes of old had to pass, it is guarded by threatening monsters. But all monsters are simply the embodiment of our own fears and once we face them courageously they will fall back, powerless to hurt us, leaving the way clear for us to pass through the gate and into the strange countries we cannot as yet see clearly.

The Moon card also shows us how the claws of the physical—the crayfish whose natural element is the primeval water from which all life has emerged—are reluctant to relinquish us. Because the world and life within it is so beautiful it is hard to want to turn away and take the path through that narrow and mysterious gate, consciously gearing ourselves to brave trials and terrors we are not sure we can face or overcome. The point of awareness of the spiritual is perhaps the point at which we are closer than ever to the physical and cling to it reluctant to let go.

During the months when I suppose I was passing through this stage myself I was living in London, trying to come to terms with my psychic potential and actively live a spiritual life. I was also struggling physically, since my health was poor and I was on heavy medication, in constant pain. The prospect of my trials continuing indefinitely was a dismal one—for often it is not the big issues but the little niggling details of physical existence that provide the 'last straw' that really breaks us.

I felt quite ready to plunge determinedly into cosmic confrontation with destiny and whatever demons I might have to overcome but I could be reduced to tears having to cope with the mundane. Climbing back-wrenchingly in and out of a car, trying to control the palpitations and panic attacks that crippled attempts to assert myself or facing up to my bloated and elderly image in a mirror had reduced me long since to confiding to a friend that I found physical existence so difficult I wished I could exist as just 'a brain on legs'.

I regularly attended the Spiritualist Church in Fulham, which like most Spiritualist Churches offers spiritual healing after the services and during the week. I was only too thankful to be able to take advantage of these sessions. They not only made me feel better and calmer but it was while they were actually taking place that spontaneously, without really believing what was happening to me, I became aware of my abilities as a medium. I started to 'see' and to receive messages from the spirit world—at first for the healers who were working on me.

I was very chary and doubtful about the visions to begin with. Since I had not been attending the Church for very long I held the mediums in high esteem and regarded the prospect of joining their ranks as an honour to which I could never hope to aspire. I did not seriously consider such a thing possible. People trained for years to develop their mediumship—so surely I was being extremely arrogant to assume I could just 'naturally' start communicating with the departed overnight, as it were?

But the messages carried on coming, though it was difficult for me to know whether or not I was somehow inducing them myself. I was aware too of the dangers of accepting apparent psychic or spiritual messages without question when you are inexperienced. What reassured me was that my development as a medium seemed to be taking place while I was actually in the Church building, in the care and under the protection of healers working for Spirit. I found later that my destined path was to be that of a kind of psychic maverick with no particular affiliations to any one formal creed, but I do not believe it was chance that my first steps into the realms of Spirit were made literally within the Church itself.

The early communications I received as a medium rooted me very firmly into the physical. At first I was given simple messages to pass on to the healers from sources they identified as departed relatives or friends, and in the traditional manner in which mediums work, several messages were accompanied by loving images of flowers. But I was not aware of any sort of 'Spirit Guide' and seemed to be able to make contact quite easily and safely without one. Then one day there was a new development. I was given the first clear message for myself from someone in Spirit whom I recognised—though I found great difficulty both in accepting his presence in any sort of mystical connection and in casting him (of all people) in the role of spiritual adviser!

Throughout my twenties I had had a ten-year relationship with a much older man who had been my colleague, mentor, lover and friend. Though one of the most vibrantly alive personalities I have ever known he was not a spiritual person—had not even believed in a god or an afterlife—but to my amazement I found it was he who was coming through during my healing sessions at the Church.

He took me back to a specific place and time that had meant a lot to me: the lovely city of Chester in the springtime of the first year we had known each other. The pink and white of flowering blossom trees had marked not only the beginning of what to me seemed the kind of fairy-story romance most people only dream about, but also the beginning of my career as a writer, which he had helped to foster and encourage.

The same presence and visions returned for some weeks, every time I went back to the Church for healing, until I was able to accept and understand the message I was being given. It was not passed on in words as such but in a way that would become very familiar to me in the future, as thought patterns entering my mind and awareness.

Everything had been before me in the springtime when we had first met. I had been young and (even if I say it myself) lovely, talented and confident in my ability to challenge fate and conquer the world. Now I was worn and tired, had just suffered the break-up of a distressing third marriage that had left me alone with no resources. Perhaps worst of all, the writing career on which my living depended was going through a bad patch.

The spirit world revealed itself to me in those early communications as first and foremost immensely practical. It also gave me evidence of how lovingly Spirit cares for all our needs.

I was not removed from the earth plane and levitated onto some kind of heavenly cloud, with a saintly being garbed in robes of wisdom appearing to guide me towards that narrow gateway and what lay beyond. I was provided instead with solid reassurance in the form of a 'man of the world' I had trusted and loved to help me in the most material of ways. Cosmic warfare and battles with the dark could not cripple me so much as my human fears and my most pressing problems—physical discomfort, lack of confidence, even the chronic state of my finances and business dealings. This particular person was the one who had 'been there' in these respects for me during the earlier blossom-time days in Chester: he was exactly the person to lift me now when I was lost and vulnerable.

This revelation in itself showed me that the concepts held by many of the spiritual as somehow very solemn and elevated, terribly serious and always, as it were, on its best behaviour could not be more inaccurate.

Once when I submitted the outline of a book I wanted to write about my psychic work I suggested that one of the chapters should focus on the irreverent levity, the wit and humour—including jokes and repartee—that I have encountered in my dealings with the spirit world. The publisher wrote back with the repressive comment that he did not think that there was any place for that sort of thing in such a book. It was obvious that he had no real knowledge of the spiritual, for a lively appreciation of humour is not something that is discarded when one passes into other realms.

Any medium can tell you that when communicating with the departed they often find the experience of dying seems to have sharpened many individuals' sense of irony and of the ridiculous, particularly if they had previously not believed there would be any kind of an afterlife. But a beginner unprepared for the encompassing completeness of spiritual actuality does not expect Spirit Guides of any sort—however dear they might have been in life—to turn up in their familiar sensual, worldly guise. The fact that 'guides' are likely to communicate in just the way they would have communicated when they were alive, even down to the odd swear word or two, comes as a refreshing surprise. Yet souls who have passed into spirit do not basically change. They have the same uniqueness, the same characteristic quirks of speech and expression, the same ways of looking at things, that marked them as individuals when they were on the Earth.

My own experience suggests that the departed have to learn when they pass into a more spiritual existence, to refine their awareness and work on their personal perceptions and values themselves. This does not automatically happen, they are not somehow transformed into angelic or saintly beings, their human faults, biases and prejudices miraculously wiped out.

I have never been able to regard my own first communicant as anything so portentous and formal as a 'Spirit Guide'—and I am quite sure that he would have considered such a title the most tremendous joke. His still-living presence with me seemed altogether so far-fetched and unlikely that it took years before I felt I could reveal to anyone else how he had come through from 'beyond the veil' with the practical help I needed so badly.

His message was—as his words had always been in life—grounding and reassuring. He told me to open my eyes, to look beyond my own personal preoccupations and stop clinging so fearfully to my state of disillusion and distress. It was actually the springtime of the year once again and the blossom trees in London were coming out—there was one in full glorious bloom outside the Church.

'Yes, that earlier time we were destined to share was beautiful, but it has gone so let it go. This Spring is just as real and this your own, it is for you. Take it and enjoy it, live in this moment. It is meant to be and though things are very different now, not what you expected, this is your time. A new blossoming, a new beginning.'

Since my very first days as a medium this particular 'guide' has stayed with me and been there whenever I have needed his humour and companionship, his practical advice and assistance. When I asked him how it was possible that he, who did not even believe in the spiritual, had come to 'be there' for me, this was the answer I received, with no further explanation.

'You needed an angel didn't you? Why shouldn't there be an angel in a grey business suit?'

Coping with our physical existence is often more difficult than trying to transcend it. Humour can help but it is easy to despair because the dark side of our human selves sometimes seems so deep and fathomless that we are afraid we will never manage to struggle free of its clutches or come to terms with it. And our attempts to do so can make up the whole story of our lives.

During the time we appear to be living as physical beings we may well be required to undertake the most incredible odysseys into worlds others are unaware of. The ancient heroes in the realms of myth and fantasy made voyages that are symbolic of the journeying of every human soul on its eternal quest for self-discovery and self-awareness. Like them, we may be engaged in gigantic battles on some other plane as we pass through dark nights of the soul on our own personal battlefields.

We may be struggling to free ourselves from deadly enchantment, slay dragons or overcome fearful monsters and the struggle can be intense, perhaps leave us wounded and with scars. Yet our daily life might appear quite uneventful—even boring—to the people around us and show no apparent sign of achievement.

I encounter many sitters who are in the same situation that I was when I went to the Spiritualist Church to try and find the help I needed so desperately. They are worn, distressed, bewildered and disheartened. They may be near breaking point, expending incredible amounts of energy and willpower simply in order to stand their ground and enable them to stay where they are.

'I don't know why I should be in this state,' they say wearily. 'I can't understand it, I am so lucky really, I ought not to be complaining.'

It is difficult for such people to put their problem into words. 'I try really hard, I struggle all the time but I can't seem to get anywhere.' Or else: 'I have always tried really hard but I never seem to make any progress.'

Displaying all the symptoms of soldiers suffering from battle fatigue, exhausted from too many campaigns and constantly on the alert as they pass through enemy territory, some individuals have long since lost sight of any actual objective at all. They do not know where they are trying to get to any longer, simply trudge on mindlessly thinking they are getting nowhere.

Alice in Lewis Carroll's *Through the Looking-glass,* found herself in just such a no-win situation when she tired herself out running what seemed to be a very long way only to discover when she stopped that she was in exactly the same spot. When she asked for an explanation the White Queen informed her breezily that: '. . . here you see, it takes all the running you can do, to keep in the same place. If you want to get somewhere else, you must run at least twice as fast as that!'

Rites of passage recognised as marking significant developments in our lives are generally celebrated publicly in our society. As well as the difficult—even traumatic— milestones, intensely happy events like weddings, the realisation of ambitions or the achieving of goals are praised as personal achievements. Even the fact that we have survived for another year is regarded as worthy of universal congratulation when our birthday comes round!

The rites of passage that take place in public do ensure that to some extent at least, others are likely to understand we are going through times when we might need support or assistance—or even just approval of, and appreciation for our efforts. But we can find ourselves setting out alone at any moment to undertake an awesome trial of strength or confronting enemy forces on some private battlefield.

The enemy may not have a physical form. It can be something intangible that others are unaware of and perhaps will never encounter themselves since their own particular path will take them in other directions.

Our enemy may actually lurk deep within our own selves, causing us to struggle against emotions we cannot control, passions that seem to rise up threatening to swamp all else. Such difficulties in overcoming emotional or behavioural problems generally arise from past experience and mistaken perceptions and they can persist throughout our lives.

Some individuals have long since surrendered to the burdens of grief or loss and seem doomed to spend their days in a kind of perpetual mourning, though not necessarily for actual people, loved ones they might miss. They may be mourning their own lost youth, lost innocence, freedom from responsibility, their own childhood days to which they can never return.

As we grow older the present can seem increasingly frightening, alien and strange, the province of new young generations to which we do not belong. Nostalgia for the past can tempt us to reject our physical reality and all it has to offer us in the now, leaving us unable to enjoy our current existence or take any pleasure in the prospect of a future.

97

One of the most common legacies of the past can be anger, whether against others, against fate, or whether we have in guilt and shame turned it inwards and are blaming ourselves. Choked down, repressed anger can wreak havoc on the person trying hard not to express it. Some of my own worst battles have been against my fear of expressing my anger as well as the anger itself. The power that seemed to be unleashed was so terrifying that I was afraid I would not survive and I tried to describe what I had just experienced after one such struggle:

It isn't just anger, it's rage, fury, boiling and seething, shaking me, every inch of me, inside and out. Murderous, vitriolic. I am helpless, at a standstill. I'm aware of nothing except this monumental living ache of feeling crashing painfully and impotently at the furthest extremities of my mind and my body. Not only fury but hate as well, so fierce, so powerful that it's like being held upright by the force that's hurtling from one part of me to another, blindly seeking escape.

It's like being in the eye of the whirlwind. If it should go away suddenly, this minute, I would fall, I couldn't stand. It's driving me, driving me so that my mind is racing ahead of time. The whole world outside seems to have slowed down, I have passed it, I'm on my way out in front somewhere.

Since our inner journeyings are often not visible to others our greatest efforts may never be recognised or appreciated by those around us. Sometimes just the effort of working ourselves up to say 'no' can take more courage and mark a greater triumph than standing up before the cannon of an army. Each of us treads his or her own unique path through life, and we never know where or when the mysterious gateways that mark our passage will appear. It is as futile to compare one person's suffering or struggle with another on a kind of Richter scale as it is to make sweeping evaluations of what each has achieved.

In the course of my own mental and spiritual journeys on the long voyage to self-discovery I spent years of struggle and anguish trying to survive apparent 'madness', addiction to the drugs I was prescribed, locked wards, learning how to cope with the fact that I was intensely psychic and half the time lived 'out of body'. Yet it might well have seemed to an observer that I achieved very little, since a great deal of the time I never even seemed to be able to function as 'normally' competent at coping or making a living.

I am not the only person who might be said (in those emotive words of the cliché) to have 'gone through hell', trying desperately in the middle of the agony to find some kind of explanation as to what it was all about. In my own case however, the pattern of events seemed at last to make some kind of possible sense when I learned more about the development of a 'wise man' or 'wise woman' and studied accounts of the process known as the 'shamanic journey'.

Descriptions of shamanic initiation in all cultures where they occur involve a period of terrifying isolation where the false self has to be utterly relinquished and the soul is torn apart by demons. The pieces are scattered to the four winds in order to enable spiritual rebirth in enlightenment and wisdom. In the commentary to the book I wrote recording my own experiences I mentioned such accounts of the 'shamanic journey' and added: 'I believe my own journey, undertaken in great personal misery and unhappiness, which led me into areas that were uncharted, unmapped, horrific and annihilating, could have been such an initiation.'

It is what I can tell them of my observations and experiences during my own journeys of self-discovery that perhaps reassure others—

people like my sitters—better than anything else I can say, that what they might be suffering and enduring is not something unique. They are not destined for some awful doom that, while missing everyone else, has somehow marked them out as victims and will destroy them. However terrible the situation in which they might find themselves, others have been there too, others have survived.

Perhaps even more important to the distressed and the suffering is the awareness that though they have to tread the path laid out for them physically on their own—whether or not they feel they have any kind of spiritual guidance— there are others who can understand what they are going through. There are individuals who have passed a similar road before them who are prepared to stand by them to offer help and encouragement. Not to fight their battles, of course, for no-one except they themselves can do that. But to strengthen their will not to give up, to give them the confidence to believe they too can emerge victorious and 'come shining through'.

Say not the struggle naught availeth,
The labour and the wounds are vain,
The enemy faints not, nor faileth,
And as things have been, things remain.

For while the tired waves, vainly breaking,
Seem here no painful inch to gain,
Far back through creeks and inlets making
Comes silent, flooding in, the main.

And not by eastern windows only,
When daylight comes, comes in the light,
In front the sun climbs slow, how slowly,
But westward, look, the land is bright.

Arthur Hugh Clough
Say Not the Struggle Naught Availeth

Chapter 5

Travelling Companions

'Is there anybody there?' said the traveller
Walter de la Mare *The Listeners*

Thou wert my guide, philosopher and friend
Alexander Pope *An Essay on Man*

A medium is usually represented—as a character in literature or even in the expectations of the modern media—as an eccentric who sits at a table in a darkened room talking to apparently empty air. This individual conducts long, jolly conversations with an unseen but exotically named 'Spirit Guide' (usually sounding like a comedy performer who missed his vocation on the stage) while other spirits that might be present are spookily requested to participate by knocking on the table—'Once for yes, twice for no!'

In my last book *In and Out the Windows*: *My Life as a Psychic* I wrote that I 'do not have a Spirit Guide as such, in some familiar form with a name'. But having given the matter some thought, I can see now that I have

103

unknowingly been as misled as everyone else by the well-worn cliché images of mediums and their 'Spirit Guides'.

As well as being given practical help from my 'angel in a grey business suit' I have in fact received a great deal of instructive guidance of an extremely elevated and widely encompassing nature as I have progressed in psychic and spiritual awareness. My advisors have been the entities, presences, angels or whatever else you like to call them who have appeared from time to time—and continue to do so—in order to offer me help, insight and information.

These are obviously 'Spirit Guides'.

But I have to admit I have never been able to regard any of the beings that have communicated with me, in whatever way, as either 'spirits' or 'guides' even though they have actually been both. This is because 'Spirit Guides' are usually perceived by the uninitiated (and you have to remember that before I learned about such matters I was uninitiated myself!) as probably rather like the popular concept of ghosts. Other-worldly and unreal. Extremely stagey. Awe-inspiring—or perhaps the opposite, physically uncomfortable, even painful to encounter. The prospect of communicating with any disembodied being that apparently 'comes through' in a darkened room while the medium is in a trance would almost inevitably appear to offer the person with no experience of such things either 'fakery or fright'.

I was to discover that there are various kinds of mediumship, that mediums and 'Spirit Guides' work in their own individual ways and that it is not always necessary to hold seances—or even go into a trance—to make contact. I do not actually require a darkened room or any other kind of formal setting to connect with the spirit world myself, I simply need to concentrate and focus my mind on what I am doing. In my ignorance and because it seemed so much less complicated than the elaborate rituals I anticipated I would have to learn, I assumed for a long time that though able to contact and interact with discarnate beings, including souls who have passed over, I could not claim to be a 'proper' medium.

The presences of which I became increasingly aware did not appear to resemble the traditional (presumably the reputable kinds of) 'Spirit Guides' claimed by other mediums I met. And they were certainly nothing at all like the formidable beings I expected who would loom apparition-like, holding forth with pronunciations I would immediately recognise as heavily significant and obviously from some other plane.

My own guiding presences emerged in the most natural way possible, almost as though they were friends I had met up with after a long absence. They did not make pronunciations of any kind but generally left the initiative to me, so our communication took the shape of informal—sometimes almost casual—chats. I was able to recognise afterwards though that in these apparently simple exchanges the most amazingly wise and deep philosophies and teachings had been imparted. Often I found myself actually laughing in appreciation of my communicants' wit and humour—as well as being enlightened I was provided with the most stimulating companionship I had ever encountered.

Though these presences exist within my own mental perceptions and nobody else is able to see them or connect with them, they have always seemed utterly real in just the same way that people I might know in a physical sense who are not there in the flesh, are real. There has never been any sense of ghostliness in my communications with other planes of existence: it seems perfectly 'normal' to me to be able to conduct them. And the entities and presences who share my journeys are more like tried and tested friends of long standing, members of a close-knit team, companions who happen to be travelling in the same direction and have come to know, love and understand each other well. I have never had the impression I was dealing with disembodied 'others' from realms alien to my own experience.

I came to realise that each person's experience of 'Spirit Guides' is different. Some mediums may well perceive their mentors as eminently awe-inspiring if this is what works best for them, but every individual is guided first and foremost to a complete and loving appreciation and acceptance of himself as he really is. In my own case, the joy of coming to know close and dearly loved companions with whom I could be as irreverent as I liked as well as appreciating their mental superiority had blinded me to the true facts. I had indeed been blessed with 'Spirit Guides' who were there to teach and instruct me—not in any rigidly accepted 'right' ways but in all the ways that were right for me.

Even though you may be aware of your 'Spirit Guides' yourself it is not easy to describe them to others who may want to know what they look like. Some psychics are granted the gift of psychic art. They may be able to create wonderful evocative pictures inspired by Spirit or else they will use their vision to 'link in' to whatever 'guide' they perceive around you and sketch or paint a portrait of the figure (sometimes figures) they see. I had a sitting with Sarah, a psychic artist I met during the early years of my career as a psychic when I was based in London, and she sent me afterwards a striking and lovely drawing best described in the note that accompanied it:

'A woman—a spirit connected to the water—mystical—part waves, part human. Has magical energies. Colours—blues, greens, mauves, pinks—her eyes are special. Shells and stones are around her neck and in her ears. Her whole image pours with energy—a very advanced spirit on a very different level.'

'Dear Dawn' (Sarah added, using the name under which I was known during the years I worked in London and the South of England) 'the above I wrote when you sat with me. I hope you enjoy having her portrait.'

This lovely drawing by Sarah has—like my 'angel'—triumphantly withstood the test of time. The image is infused with all the qualities I associate with Sirona, a Romano-Celtic goddess of healing who made herself known to me quite early in my spiritual searching. I began to received powerfully beautiful 'channelled' messages and texts, some of which I have included in my books, that I was able to identify as from a 'goddess' source.

Just as some individuals are drawn to one particular saint they regard as particularly relevant and inspirational to them, so I feel Sirona—an obscure and little known deity—is my own particular goddess figure. She reflects all the mysteries and secrets that were nurtured by my own Celtic background, that subtle web of poetry, magic and shimmering green paganism of which I was aware as a child. She was a water divinity and her shrines were connected with healing pools and springs—as a healer myself I relate to this aspect of her.

This was how she described herself in one of her 'channelled' communications:

> *I am the goddess of the silver spring who led the unicorn by a thread of crimson safely through the tangled thickets of the forest and before whom the giant babe-eater Behemoth (gnashing his teeth as he screamed his misery to the stars, hiding their sacred fires) knelt to kiss the tip of my robe. Prostrate he lay and from the dark hole of his mouth streamed the black slime of the knowledge of evil and upon the water near alighted a white swan, to fade like a wraith of loveliness into the dusk, and the night darkened.*

Sirona's presence, like that of my 'angel', provided me with the kind of grounding that gave me a foothold, as it were, in the new world I was to inhabit. She did not communicate with me very much after the first few years—presumably she had imparted what was necessary to my development at that time in her 'channelled' texts. But I still have Sarah's portrait, which continues to remain an inspiration.

Two other presences that came and went very briefly gave me more insight into the diversity of help and guidance I might be granted as and when I needed assistance. Before I studied Reiki I worked as a natural healer as well as a psychic and sometimes I used to feel a male presence, very authoritative and powerful, taking over my hands when I touched the patient's body. I still have no idea of 'his' identity but I sensed an arctic environment, intense cold with snow and ice and had the impression this spirit had previously lived in Alaska or somewhere else in the far North. I called him 'the Eskimo Doctor'.

Another highly colourful entity made itself known only once, very early on when I was still in the process of making contact with possible 'Spirit Guides'. I have never known whether this particular being was a man or a woman. I sensed the presence of a male personality rather than a female but when I asked for a name I was given 'Cassandra'—the prophetess who in Greek myth foretold the fall of Troy.

The story goes that the god Apollo fell in love with Cassandra and promised her the gift of prophecy if she would yield to his advances. She said yes and the gift was granted but she then perversely changed her mind and refused him. The frustrated Apollo warned her that though she would indeed be able to prophesy truthfully, as a punishment for going back on her word her prophecies would never be believed.

This is not an altogether uncommon fate for those who 'see' and try to share their visions and I wondered if perhaps my uncertainty over 'Cassandra's' identity underlines the point that regardless of their sex, anyone speaking the unwelcome truth about what is to come can find themselves regarded as a 'doom and gloom' merchant.

'Cassandra' certainly seemed to be preoccupied with doom—and with a capital D! He or she only held one long 'conversation' with me and in spite of my efforts I was never able to contact him or her again. But the conversation was extremely interesting since it had something to say about a subject most responsible people find it difficult to make sense of—the distressing evils that appear to prevail within our world.

'Cassandra's' words reflect the sort of outrage and disgust we all feel sometimes but they remind us that all things work their way through, everything passes its destined course. The tragedies we think are more than we can stand, the blows that seem to mark the end of our world have happened before and will happen again—this is the concept of cyclic progression most spiritual teachings present. Even the most wonderful moments cannot last. There has to be a constant forward movement to hold the balance between the polarities, between positive and negative, good and evil.

From the 'Cassandra' text:

I found myself in a time and a place where there was idolatry of the loud and the crass and the nihilistic and the minds of the multitudes like lemmings rushed without awareness to their destruction. The end of the world has come as it came then to me and to those around me. O if only the very stones of Ninevah and Crassia and Poseidon could speak, they would cry out and say that in the midst of the sound there is only the hollow rattle of approaching death, and the skull shakes as a gourd and rattles. For there comes a time when the spirit has flickered so low that the flame is almost extinguished, and it is then that the multitude rattles together and the sound is like a torment that beats the light into madness and death.

What shall be done, and what could they do?

O without delay, seek the stony place and the bleak and bare path that is empty and where there is no sound, and hold the moment and the stillness. O weep not, nor cry where shall we go, for the stony place is within, and the path beneath the feet of every spirit.

O let the viands of filthiness and pigs swilling their troughs go, and see that even the pigs are creatures of inner clean, and see rather the lowest of predators snorting in their rotting remains and in the excrement and vomit, and, unaware, saying: This is richness. Lift the stained snout from such outrage in the face of the flames of divinity, and kneel for the drops of living water.

O like the water to a soul that is at the moment of extinction is the peace of the stony place, and to me. Many times I came to this moment, to the lifting of my head to see the multitudes illuminated in the sulphurous flames of a living hell, their blues and reds, and I saw them and stood among them and said: How came I here, and wherefore?

I am sick with the old, old sickness that again I must stand to watch the death throes of the god flames, and I ask why, o why must this be so? It is so far from the pearls of living water, the coolness and smoothness, the essence of purity and stillness.

Spiritual teachings sometimes need to be uncomfortably couched in language that will hit home. If we will not confront the truth—however upsetting—and face the real reasons why we need reassurance and comfort, we can never be realistically comforted.

We have seen that life seems to provoke the same questions 'Cassandra' asks so passionately: why does ugliness and horror exist, why are terrible things allowed to happen, why must living break our hearts? Some things are so hurtful that they seem to rub out all sense of the beautiful and the good. How is it possible to live, to want to live when we must accept the extremes of evil, depravity and cruelty that exist?

Alongside the questions the answer is also given. It is up to each individual soul to make its own decision about the reality in which it will choose to live, what it will value and recognise and uphold. But 'Cassandra' perhaps speaks for all of us in asking 'How?' and 'Why?' and 'What for?'

There was more in this interview that I found extremely thought-provoking:

I am the watcher at the gate of hell. I am the one granted the vision too late to be believed. I was called at one time, Cassandra. I wept and tore my hair, and gave my own flame to help the others, but they have no ears and I learned it was useless. I do not come until the rattle is in the throat and death is imminent. I am the Mourner for I feel for the pity and the waste, and I am the Light Bearer to be there when the rattles cease and the small god flames turn in fearful bewilderment and look for assistance.

I asked: Is this hell then, here and now?

What else? Hell is not a place to which the soul goes, it is a place which comes and seeks admittance and is received joyously and makes its home within the head and the heart. And hell is not cruelty and pain, it is the slow eroding away of all that makes up the god light; it is blankness and the eroding of all true sensation of the mind so that there is no difference between the things of seeming richness and the offal.

For there walk among the sheep many beasts with ravening jaws slobbering blood, and no man sees or knows, and the laughter is the same for each death as for the coloured balls spinning in the air.

'Cassandra's' highly emotive pronunciations can seem frightening (as well as incomprehensible) to minds unused to prophetic utterance and fire-and-brimstone oratory. I usually refer sitters who are lost in dread and despair to the easier to understand parallels we can draw from the tarot card called the Ten of Swords.

This indicates the heaviest of all burdens that have to be carried in life, the sort of thing that can seem like a real 'end of our world' where everything is lost and nothing can get any worse. But when you are as low as you can be and have faced the worst possible scenario there is, the future actually appears quite cheerful by comparison. There is only one way left to go and that is—up!

There are no inflexible rules about 'Spirit Guides'. They can be of any kind and they may come and go, appearing as and when they are needed. The individual progressing along his spiritual path grows in awareness and maturity and will be given the guidance that is relevant to that specific time and moment in his development. It does seem though that everybody is given one (occasionally more) particular 'Spirit Guide' who is especially personal and who remains more or less constant.

In my book *In and Out the Windows: My Life as a Psychic* I explained how when I began consciously trying to live a spiritual life and connect with whatever spiritual guidance I was to be given, I became aware first of two tiny, loving little spirits I called 'Blue and Stalk'. They prepared me, unaccustomed as I was then to any kind of spiritual communication, to accept presences and entities around me as part of my everyday living. I assumed at first that these were to be my 'official Spirit Guides' since they were obviously from some higher plane and not, like the 'Eskimo Doctor' and 'Cassandra', the departed spirits of people who had lived on Earth.

There are supposedly differences between the spirits of those who have passed over and entities originating on higher (or possibly deeper?) levels but I have never tried to classify or catalogue them. Whatever dogmatic assumptions I might have been tempted to hold have generally only proved to reveal how inadequate as well as unnecessary they are. I plodded on trying to have faith, and a few years after my psychic career had begun I wrote more about my early encounters with my 'guides':

In a changing world when my whole physical and mental existence was moving in directions I had not been able to anticipate or imagine, it seemed I had nothing to cling to except for my links with Spirit. But though these brought me great joy and unbelievable happiness and peace, I was to find what I had, in my secret heart, always suspected and feared, that neither happiness nor peace is static. They are attitudes, ways of life rather than gifts, and must be worked at. One constantly needs to replenish one's faith, optimism and positivity or they will run low and the dark of negativity will come flooding in.

Most philosophies teach that there are only two states of being—fear and love. They cannot exist simultaneously, and the presence of one will cancel out the other. As I was starting to work towards what I hoped would prove to be the dawning of my spiritual maturity I tried with all my might to cling only to love and wipe out my fears, but dark worries, doubts, suspicions, jealousies and insecurities are as persistent as gnats in a swarm. Even now I am still trying. (I have learned that this process never ends.)

118

In the early days I clung to the two 'Little Spirits,' who had revealed themselves to me, and was comforted by the beauty of the mental images I received from them of a silver and blue 'Star' plane where I could rest and gather my strength for what was to come. Revelations of the 'Star' plane opened up other dimensions and worlds during my meditations but at first I made my mental journeys alone. Apart from the 'Little Spirits', which looked like tiny sparks of light, I saw no other Spirit Guide and I encountered no 'soul mate' or 'dream lover', even though I was by this time working with other psychics who said they had.

One evening I was feeling particularly low and isolated from the rest of the world. I prayed with a desperate longing in my heart for some further help and comfort. The time had obviously come when I was ready to meet my own truest guide in the spirit—and that was when I first became aware of Mist.

Who or what Mist is, I am not sure. Teacher, inspiration, counsellor, companion, comforter —Mist has been and is all these so far as I am concerned. But whether 'he' is a self-contained entity or a part of myself, as some teachings would have us believe, I do not know or need to know.

Whether 'he' is actually my own Higher Self, the missing masculine part of my identity instead of the wise and steadying other 'he' seems is irrelevant.

'He' remains my link with the Source, the guiding presence that has been with me since the early days of my psychic awareness in some form or another, far more meaningful and 'real' to me than any physical being. My 'angel' relates to me on a practical level but Mist has accompanied me not only through the mysterious moonlit gateway into the realms of the spirit but into the furthest dimensions of infinity beyond.

Perhaps I should explain here that though I generally refer to Mist in the masculine, 'he' (like all spiritual beings) actually has no physical sex as such and it would be more correct to refer to him as 'it'. Any discussion of the kind of closeness a medium experiences with a 'Spirit Guide' is difficult to convey, however, except by using the traditional cliché terms in which one would refer to the most intimate partnership or relationship.

I became aware over a period of years that my personal 'Spirit Guide' is actually formless, a sort of swirling silver cloud of the pure spiritual energy from which 'his' name originates. When I asked what 'his' name was—who 'he' was—the reply was a factual pointing out that 'he' was nobody, he was nothing except that spirit and that energy.

'I am mist.'

It is for the sake of convenience only that I always refer to 'him' as a masculine individual with a name, 'he' and 'Mist'. One of the characteristics of Spirit is that it can present itself in whatever form seems appropriate at any given time and when I first became aware of Mist it was not as disembodied energy. I was obviously not ready and had not progressed enough to relate simply to a vision of silver light but was presented with a definite entity in a shape I could identify, that of a figure I took to be a man.

The figure seemed to be wearing silvery armour something like that worn by a knight of old, though it did not appear stiff or heavy. It was completely encasing and I could not at first see the face. I seemed to be looking at the figure from an angle where the face was not visible—though later the angle shifted but the face was still obscured by the visor that covered the head and formed part of the armour.

This outline of a man's figure with a definable shape had been presented to me, I learned, to make my awareness of 'his' presence easier.

121

The 'silver man with no face' became familiar and dear to me but later, though the presence was still as powerful, the image in which it revealed itself varied. For many years now it has been —and is—just the energy, the 'Mist'.

But at first I was unaware of all this. I related to a 'silver man', the actual nature of my 'guide' becoming apparent only by degrees. When after some time I asked whether I might see 'his' face and the visor was lifted, there was no face visible as such. The visor was empty with only the impression of an image that seemed to resemble rippling or moving water. This was my introduction to the formless swirling 'mist' that is the spiritual energy's natural state.

In telepathic communication that required no words or explanation, the presence of 'Mist' gave me the reassurance of cosmic love, comfort and awareness I needed and had glimpsed in my mystical 'Near Death' type of experience years before. 'He' has remained with me ever since, providing wisdom and counsel, keeping me constantly in touch with the higher spiritual levels and continuing to advise and teach me.

I have always been aware of the presence of Mist as incredibly powerful but I was surprised and gratified to find it could also be apparent to other people and affect them strongly. A healer called Ray who like Sarah was another of my early co-workers, used to regularly give me healing when we happened to have a spare half-hour or so at Psychic Fairs. I was always glad to try out the different therapies demonstrated at fairs and learn more about them, since throughout the ten or so years I worked in the South of England I was constantly in some degree of pain or distress from various ailments, including severe back trouble.

One day after Ray had finished giving me healing he told me he had perceived some significant presence with me during the session. I asked him to write his impressions down as a record and this is what he wrote:

'Whilst giving healing to Dawn today I saw clairvoyantly with her a spiritual entity in the form of outstretched arms turned upwards carrying a huge sphere of blue/white— white/blue light which I find almost impossible to describe. The entire sphere projected its light in the form of fluid rays onto Dawn, engulfing her entirely.

'A feeling of deep awe, respect, humility and especially joy and upliftment overcame me. Dawn recognised this highly evolved Entity as MIST.

123

'His message was that Dawn needs to visualise him and contact him on a daily basis for the replenishment of both her spiritual and physical beings thus giving her healing and harmony.'

When Ray described the 'entity' he had seen I recognised it at once. All the qualities this vision inspired, as well as the power of the image and the description of the silver/blue light was pure 'Mist' and I was thrilled that someone else had been able to perceive and relate to 'his' purity and strength.

But Ray was not the only person to present me with an independent picture of Mist. For years I treasured a drawing in crayon done by a psychic artist called Sharon, whom I had encountered in one of the very early venues where I had worked as a psychic. I only attended this venue a few times. I did not care for it since the atmosphere and the way in which it was run had a strange and unsettling kind of energy much more geared to control-freaking and the materialistic rather than the spiritual. But it was the very fact that this was such an unlikely source of true vision that made the result of my sitting with Sharon so surprising.

At the time I was still finding it difficult to believe in my spiritual destiny, still suffering from many doubts. Though I accepted Mist with all my heart it was difficult to relate this subtle, disembodied presence to the more identifiable 'Spirit Guides' of other psychics and mediums. I sometimes wondered—as one is inclined to do—whether I was actually imagining the whole thing, creating the scenario of a spiritual destiny myself out of my own arrogance and self-importance, whether I was a true medium or some kind of fake.

Particularly did these doubts arise with regard to the ways in which I was able to communicate with the worlds beyond that mysterious moonlit gateway. I could not help feeling I might be making assumptions about my own ability to make independent contact that would lead me to a nasty fall. Other psychics seemed to work more traditionally with guides who were 'real'—I saw many psychic portraits of them, often extremely detailed and nearly always lovely. Beautiful goddess and priestess figures, imposing Native American Indians, regal men of wisdom from ancient China or Japan, even clear-eyed people in white robes and crowns from Atlantis. Their very names rang with authority. Running Deer—Nimatu—Cherapakim.

Rather childishly, I longed for a similar portrait of my own guide though I recognised my 'want' as an unnecessary whim and had resigned myself rather glumly to the fact that I was unlikely to get such a picture. Would any artist be inspired to sketch a grey-white blank that represented a fog?

But when Sharon offered to undertake a portrait of my 'Spirit Guide', I accepted the offer and sat down with her. I had told her nothing about Mist and wondered what she would perceive. I was prepared to be disappointed and fully expected her to draw some kind of authority figure that resembled the 'guides' of the other psychics.

Sharon was still gaining experience—as unsure in her way as I was in mine. She made a few strokes with her pencil, frowning, and after a while she paused.

'It's a bit odd. I said I would draw your guide, and I do have a picture forming in my mind but it isn't really a guide. It isn't even a person and you will think it's very peculiar. I don't know whether I should try and link in to something else—.'

'Oh no, draw exactly what you see,' I told her. 'It doesn't matter what it looks like, but please don't try to make it into anything else, Sharon.

Put it down just as it is.'

When she showed me the finished picture I was thrilled and amazed though she was still inclined to be rather apologetic.

'I hope you don't mind—.'

'Mind?' I said. 'Mind? You've no idea how wonderfully accurate you are. This is exactly what my "Guide" is like.'

She had drawn a silver-white sphere rather like the popular image of a flying saucer, with rays projecting from it onto the rim of a planet below, all in delicate shades of silver and grey.

'I don't know what it means, but it's what came into my mind for you,' she explained and I told her of Ray's description of Mist, adding:

'It's incredible, but although this might look like something out of science fiction— Invaders from Mars or the Body Snatchers— you have captured the essence of Mist for me, even though I couldn't have begun to describe "him" to you.'

It is due to Mist that I have progressed in learning to achieve whatever wisdom and spiritual insight I may possess. I have held two-way discussions, conversations and exchanges with 'him' over the years that are written down and stored in various binders and folders—for I am reluctant to throw any of my records of Mist's communications away. Apart from containing teaching to which I can return again and again when I need counsel they also provide a comprehensive account of my development in awareness and learning. My questions and the answers I was given form a sort of descriptive manual of the task to which I was called and the training I had to undertake to prepare myself as a 'wise woman'. Like the 'shamanic journey' this is probably a broadly similar process for all those who might have the calling and the vocation.

The records reflect all the aspects—even the most trivial and silly—of my problems in trying to advance along my path. The student is constantly hampered by the limitations of his human frailty and is constantly having to be reminded of lessons he thought he had long since learned but now finds he has forgotten. One of my own most recurring preoccupations has been my attempt to come to terms with my fear of physical pain. Here is a short extract from one of my many conversations with Mist on the subject of physical suffering:

Should we not fear pain and illness?
Fear has its part to play, otherwise there would be no fear.
What about pain and illness?
Do you experience them now?
No, not at this moment. I am concentrating on the conversation. Not unless I look for them, I suppose.
There is your answer.
But we do experience pain, I know I did when I had surgery—and the time I had very bad toothache. It was agonising, sometimes unbearable. What should we do then?
You bore it and survived.
I can remember it though. It did exist.
So did birth.
That is a strange thing to say.
Why so? Birth is your greatest suffering.
You mean, if we had not been born, we would not have to suffer at all?
Even so.
Well, I suppose that's true. We would not be human. But are we sent here only to suffer?
To survive it and so overcome it.
Death will be a release, then?
An unlocking of the prison door.
But why, Mist? What is our life for? What is human existence all about?
To question.
Is that necessary?
Nothing is stationary. All progresses.

From where, to where?
(Silence)
I suppose you won't tell me.
If I told you, would you be any better off?
No, I suppose not, but I'd know, at least.
Knowledge is not an end in itself.
What about truth?
Truth IS. Knowledge assists.

Within the last few years two other individual guiding presences have made themselves known to me and joined my particular 'team' or 'company'—or more accurately, they have allowed me the privilege of joining theirs. Brother Gregory, a 12th Century Augustinian monk, first introduced himself with messages for my partner, Paul. He continued to give me 'channelled' teaching of great simplicity and holiness based on his own love of the natural world and love of God, some of which have appeared in other books I have written. His words about the spiritual journey are included further on at the end of Chapter Seven.

Brother Gregory first brought the atmosphere, the scents and sunlight of a mediaeval abbey garden in the South of England into my awareness while I was sitting in a coffee shop in the King's Road in London. Strangely enough, though I now live in the North West Midlands it was also in London that my most recently acquired 'Guide' made contact when I was spending a few days with my friend Rosemarie, a psychic medium who is also a Reiki healer as well as a qualified reflexologist.

Rosemarie has for some time had a Native American Indian among her 'Spirit Guides', and sitters who consult her at her home have told her they have 'seen' Native American Indians in the room even though they do not consider themselves particularly psychic. I have always secretly been inclined to regard a Native American 'Guide' as very much a cliché image even though I have studied their culture and traditions spasmodically over the years and for some time possessed a 'storyteller ring' of Navajo silver and turquoise that I was actually wearing on my hand when completing my First Degree Reiki attunement. I have also had a vivid recollection of a previous existence in which I was a young American Indian girl who was wearing a white buckskin dress and seemed to be taking part in some significant ceremony where I was immersed in water and almost drowned. On the whole though, I have found the Native American Indian culture difficult to accept wholeheartedly even though it is similar in many ways to the ancient Celtic—extremely physical, realistic and if necessary brutal as well as highly spiritually evolved.

I was sleeping overnight on a mattress on Rosemarie's living room floor, just settling down when I became aware myself of a Native American Indian in the room with me. He seated himself cross-legged beside me in the manner of someone keeping a watch as I drifted to sleep. The next morning he was still there. When I told Rosemarie she was unsurprised.

'He has come to take care of you,' she assured me, though why I suddenly needed a bodyguard I did not know. 'He will go with you when you leave.'

And so he did. I was amused to find that though no-one else on the coach home could see him, he was sitting with folded arms on the seat next to mine. Since then I have found he is around if I need him but mainly he appears when I am working with Reiki. He works with me, sometimes taking over my hands as the 'Eskimo doctor' used to do. On other occasions I am aware of him carrying out his own healing rituals alongside me, in the process of which I am given vivid images of the way he viewed his country, the landscape and the animals of North America. I also receive insight into the methods used by his tribe for healing.

I have not yet managed to discover the tribe to

which he belonged but his name is Red Elk. There is a kind of shamanic link with another, much older member of his tribe too, but this man does not reveal himself fully. I am aware of the still figure sitting quietly cross-legged in the shadows, too frail to walk but radiating spiritual power. Because the name I get for him is Grey Elk I assume these two were probably related—perhaps Grey Elk was a shaman, a medicine man who passed his teachings on to his son or grandson.

Though I would love to know more about them I am content to wait until they decide to let me discover further details in their own time. I feel highly honoured and grateful they are with me.

They help me to stay grounded in the physical that I have always found so difficult to accept; and through the merging of my being and reality with theirs I can see how clearly we are all—whether in the spirit or in the flesh—a part of each other.

The principles of Reiki illustrate this beautifully. 'Rei-ki' is the Japanese for the source of healing that is recognised in all cultures under many different names. Whatever the name it is the same thing—the 'life force', the 'God-light', the 'Spirit', that pure stream of life energy that flows abundant and eternal, sustaining and containing us all.

Though the seas overflow and the rivers burst their banks yet many waters cannot quench us for we are indestructible and in our weakness is our strength. Upon our brows we carry the stars and the moons are beneath our feet. As the eternal rocks are a part of each other, so our handclasp will wear away only in aeons of winter rain and the droughts of summer. We are indivisible for there is no seam and the fabric was woven by one loom.

We are a garden of flowers of which there are many blooms yet all are enclosed within the same high wall. We are the colours in a prism of light that are all different and dart their separate ways and can never meet or be the same and yet are part of the whole. We have died separately so that we may know what it is to live, together.

We shall go forward together and still the waters to make a path. We shall read the stones and place the patterns of the clouds and the rippling of the rivers together so that all will be clear. We shall open the gates.

Channelled from *The Notta Manuscript*

Chapter 6

The Rainbow Bridge

'Death is nothing but waiting on a station platform between trains'
attributed to Dion Fortune

'Let me assert my firm belief that the only thing we have to fear is fear itself'
Franklin Delano Roosevelt

Possessing a healthy sense of fear shows we are realistically aware of the physical and mental dangers we might encounter as we go through our lives. Whatever the clichés and maxims say about bravery and cowardice and however we stiffen our spines in the determination that 'I won't show it, I won't let people know', everyone at some time or another is likely to be seriously afraid. If they are not the chances are they are temperamentally unbalanced, psychologically unsound.

Yet like pain, fear is there to be of use to us, a tool to assist in our survival. It offers challenge, a heightened state of awareness, the ability to draw on ordinarily unavailable physical strengths. It warns that there is reason to be ready to defend or to attack. It is not intended to intimidate or paralyse us beyond the limits of our endurance. When this happens, something has gone badly wrong.

Extreme fear—of whatever kind, whether some terrifying neurotic phobia or an insidious anxiety or dread—can sometimes walk with us through life like a dark shadow, poisoning the present and reaching long tentacles into the future. There may appear to be no reason for such intense feelings, they may have no recognisable roots in our current existence. We do not know why we are afraid but—as with Kate and her button phobia—our irrational terror may be crippling our lives.

In spite of all the sophisticated theories experts offer to explain away the origins of traumatisation in this life there do seem to be some cases where our fears simply cannot be accounted for. They are out of all proportion, they seem almost to have an existence of their own. Where have such extreme emotional reactions come from? It is no wonder that enquirers are inclined to feel the answer must lie outside their current existence and begin to look into the far distant past, making efforts to explore previous lives they might have lived in order to find answers and explanations.

Before I started working as a psychic I was

inclined to doubt the concept of karma. I actually knew very little about the religious aspects of it but found bland explanations put forward by people I met who were 'into' New Age culture rather superficial. I considered their glib generalisations a cop-out from serious consideration of the possible truth and significance of the subject.

It seemed far too easy to claim some individual was having to suffer from crippling arthritic pain as a punishment for torturing victims on the rack in a past life as a member of the Inquisition. Or that another was afraid of water because he had been a sailor who had gone down with his ship and drowned in an earlier existence. Or that birthmarks or physical defects were the result of having been maimed or injured in previous incarnations. Such explanations I considered so trite as to be insulting to my intelligence and I could not see the point anyway if they were regarded as simply ends in themselves. In spite of the fact that past life regression was supposedly therapeutic it was not at all clear to me how the therapy could be applied if karma was involved.

You can only speak with any authority about what you personally know. You cannot learn experience or first-hand knowledge from a book, the only way is to draw on your own sense of reality and truth. And you can never force your realities onto others, simply live them yourselves. If they are valid other people will recognise their validity and want to learn about them and absorb them from you and the way you express your values and beliefs.

All the work I have done as a psychic, all my journeys into other realms and worlds of spirit have been based on the assumption that in the end I had to find out for myself. Inevitably though, my findings have not always seemed to agree with other people's accounts or theories.

When this happens in the normal learning process the novice is inclined at first to doubt his own experience. He will be tempted to follow the advice or explanations of authorities who appear to have been proved rather than his own dubious impressions: and it is even more tempting when you are a novice in the realms of the psychic and the spiritual. If your whole aim is to let go the ego it does seem as though you are defeating the object as well as being extremely arrogant if you assume you know better than everyone else. Shouldn't you be listening humbly to the teachings of those great brains and scholars, the theorists who have worked everything out, the pioneers who have already gone this way and can tell you all about it?

As a writer I learned the habit of doing thorough background research yet always thinking a subject through for myself. But if you wander off along your own byways, make your own explorations, follow what you think are new and original methods of evaluation of the evidence and draw your own conclusions, you discover that an odd thing happens. When you have actually stepped out on your own and recklessly dismissed the teachings of others, forging ahead yourself to draw up your own blueprint, grasp the true scheme of things, assemble your personal model of the universe—you suddenly discover that it has all been done before. You have simply found another way of expressing what the great minds were saying to you in the first place.

Teachers of any sort will recognise this phenomenon—and it is the same with spiritual understanding. All belief systems lead in the end to the same god-head, the same source. All truth is exactly the same however it is expressed. When I queried the concept of karma as a governing factor in our lives, dismissing what was presented piecemeal from many sources reliable and unreliable and concentrating instead on the evidence of my own experience, very similar patterns eventually emerged to the ones I had previously been reluctant to accept.

Past-life regression cases of which I have personal experience do indicate that our attitudes, emotional responses and behaviour can be influenced by lives we have lived before this one, sometimes extremely strongly. But it is not so much what we have experienced in past life that affects us, as what we might have previously experienced regarding dying and death. It seems that death, whether some actual death in a previous life or the prospect of the physical death that currently lies ahead of us, is at the root of a great deal of the fear we experience in our present existence.

Birth and death, the two gateways by which we enter and leave this world, are equally hazardous and potentially traumatic for the spirit that is passing in or out of a physical body. Recent medical investigations into the individual's recollections and impressions of birth as well as evidence that has been accumulating for years from psychics and practitioners who conduct past-life regression seem to indicate that birth is probably more traumatic than death. So since we have all been born we have actually already safely negotiated the hardest part of our journey through life.

We rarely consider what traumas could arise from being born since we cannot remember what happened when our birth occurred and we do not anticipate another. No, the gateway that all too clearly looms ahead is a grimmer one. It is the prospect of death that is likely to haunt us—though not so much death itself as its many aspects and the ramifications that surround it.

Human beings are the only creatures who have the ability to anticipate the future. This can be a wonderful gift, allowing enjoyment in advance of pleasures to come but it can also prove a great burden. We are made aware of the inevitability of all the things we desperately fear and do not want to happen—the worst being of course, that sooner or later we are going to die. Everything involved in our physical existence will at some given moment, at a signal we know nothing about, simply stop just like that. The unthinkable will have happened. We will have come to an end.

Many of the fears we have to face up to in our lives do actually seem to be directly connected with the prospect of physical death. Anxieties about old age, loneliness, pain, disease, even the loss of loved ones hide a much deeper fear, that of our own mortality. It is the one thing about living we simply cannot swallow—for after all it does not actually make sense. It seems to contradict everything life stands for, all it is about. While we offer congratulations on a birth we proffer condolences and sympathy at a death. It is generally regarded as the complete antithesis of life, the most extreme state of 'dis-ease' or 'un-wellness' that can befall us, to be avoided at all costs.

I remember once hearing an earnest evangelical preacher exhorting his audience to live their lives with their deathbed constantly in mind, which I thought then a distinctly negative attitude. Now I can see what he meant.

Death is like all the other rites of passage, one more fence we have to jump in the great steeplechase of life. We prepare ourselves (or are prepared by others) for the frightening exhilaration of our first day at school, our important exams, our first interview, new job, engagement, wedding—and so on—yet we cringe away from that last and most challenging fence of all. A successful death should be regarded as an achievement rather than a tragedy. We can disgrace ourselves and barely make it, scrambling ignominiously through or we can transcend the barrier in one glorious, triumphant leap, really 'going for gold' and soaring over and off into the record books.

I first came face to face with human death after years of being shielded from it, as a child by my parents and later when I was an adult, by my own cowardice. Even when I had begun to work as a medium and regularly communicated with the spirits of those who had passed I had still not encountered a physically dead human body. Sometimes this bothered me, though what I might have eventually done about it I do not know—the matter was, however, taken out of my hands. Visiting a friend in Ireland I was unexpectedly rushed off with her on my arrival to attend 'a Wake'.

It was a revelation. In spite of the family's grief and my own timorous sense of apprehension there was nothing about my meeting with death but a great sense of reassurance and release. As I made my respects to the corpse who was propped up in her best dress in her own front room, holding her rosary beads in her hands I knew with the utmost certainty that all was well. She had gone home and there was no need to weep for her.

On previous occasions I had been aware of the same intuitive sense of rightness and peace— almost joy—when in the presence of relatives who were terminally ill but felt rather guilty about my reactions, thinking I must lack proper feeling, reproaching myself for being uncaring and callous. After my visit to Ireland I was reassured. Death has no sting, no weapons at all only the weapons we give it ourselves with our own fear.

As a psychic and medium I am so very aware of other planes of existence that it is this one, the physical world we inhabit that seems unlikely and limited by comparison. My physical being seems far more of an illusion to me than my awareness of a spiritual identity. But whichever way we view our existence, when the question arises of how we pass from one world into the other we are nearly all— even if we are mediums—likely to approach the concept of death with a biased or blinkered attitude.

I heard people in psychic and spiritual circles make claims that did not seem to agree at all with what I began to experience as a medium myself. It seemed to be generally assumed for instance, that people who had died certain kinds of deaths would need time to settle in on the 'other side' although there appeared to be no fixed rules. Some authorities categorically insisted that weeks—even months—should be allowed to pass before any attempt was made to contact the recently departed so I was rather disconcerted to find myself making contact with souls who had only just 'crossed over' or being aware they were making contact with me.

Some were not yet buried and one very jovial gentleman who made his appearance at a Psychic Fair (in spirit, of course) wanted me to pass on a message to his niece about how much he was looking forward to his own funeral. Whether I or the sitters were concerned that it might be 'too soon' to contact the dead it appeared they were far more resilient than seemed to be generally thought and were likely to communicate unencumbered by formalities of etiquette on their own terms.

I discovered that many recently departed individuals do look forward with enthusiasm to their funerals and that some spirits make contact easily almost as soon as they have passed. Even in cases where it is claimed the dead will require a long period of rest and recuperation—very gruesome accidents, for example—I have known them turn up apparently unscathed within a very short space of time.

My personal experience of working as a medium suggests that the physical condition of the body at death is far less relevant than the attitudes held by and mental state of the individual when alive. And for survivors worried about the wellbeing of loved ones who suffered pain or a long illness before they died, I have had repeated evidence that the spirits regard such things as in the nature of some sort of vague dream they can hardly remember.

In the process of writing this chapter I encountered a case that illustrates this in a particularly inspiring way. I was consulted by a woman whose lover had been brutally murdered only seven days previously. The police were investigating the crime and all the relevant medical procedures still being carried out. It would obviously be some time before the body was handed over to relatives. Yet when at my sitter's request I made contact with her lover he was present almost immediately to reassure her that 'I'm here, I'm all in one piece'.

She was instructed lovingly to let go the burden of the dreadful death and its attendant traumatic problems rather as though she was being shown how to unsling a rucksack from her shoulders. Her lover showed me a cobbled street and the lit lamp above the steps of an old-fashioned type of Police Station and was gently insistent that she should actually lay her burden down on the steps while he was present to watch her.

'They will deal with it,' he said. 'That is what they are there for. Leave it to them.'

The fact that the Police Station was an old-fashioned one was to subtly indicate the long tradition of the police force as dedicated to the upholding of law and order. But in a low-key, methodical manner rather than the spectacularly dramatic way in which the police are often represented in the modern media. I found this—as my sitter did—a particularly reassuring message under the circumstances since it was coming from a victim of the most unprovoked and extreme violence.

The lover appeared unaffected in any negative way by the brutal manner of his death. He was not interested in expressing feelings of revenge or even voicing what would have been an entirely understandable need to have his murderer punished. I could see that he had achieved great spiritual maturity and had a true understanding of the laws of divine and cosmic justice. When my sitter asked who had committed the crime, he told her to concern herself only with sending the perpetrator compassion. I felt he must have been a remarkable individual in life though possibly the depths of his inherent love towards mankind might not have been visibly obvious in the way he had lived.

The causes of our fears regarding death are personal to each of us and are based on fears of physical living that are dictated by experience reaching back into pasts we cannot remember. As with all negativity the fear we carry from the past breeds and feeds on itself, creating yet more fear in the present.

Cases I have personally encountered seem to indicate that our personal fears have built up over past lives as well as in this one, and will continue to increase if we let them, snowballing to cause yet deeper negative emotions to become entrenched within our personalities. Particularly relevant are the fears that result from problems we might have experienced when dealing with previous deaths in other existences.

The spirit will always pass peacefully if left to do this naturally on its own. Animals and the lower order of creatures have no rational (or irrational) emotional blocks to prevent their deaths being anything but serene in the sense that they are able to accept whatever happens to them as valid, however physically painful. The mechanism of passing always works smoothly unless something is allowed to get caught in the works and interfere with it.

In the case of human beings it is the experience of previous fear and anticipation of more which, already present within the personality, builds up and clogs the mechanism, stopping it from working. I have

148

encountered many cases where the subjects have apparently—like Kate—been 'stuck' in previous past death unable to let it go. And the chances are that unless positive action is taken to break the circle of fear and negativity ever-present somewhere in the background, it will only continue to increase in intensity as death and pain are fearfully anticipated in the individual's current existence.

It is not actual death we are afraid of. But the possible permutations of painful circumstances that can surround it can reach crushing proportions if we allow ourselves to dwell on them. And there is something far more subtly sinister inherent in the prospect of physical death—the potential threat to our sense of personal identity.

Belief in any higher power allows a relinquishing of final decisions and responsibilities in the reassuring faith that one will somehow or another probably be taken care of. But if there is no faith in a higher power there will always be an underlying fear of the threat of possible elimination of the ego, the sense not only of the self but also of the will, the ability to control. If there is no belief in anything after death then supposedly the self, the identity we have lived with throughout this life, will simply disappear when we die and go out like a candle flame.

149

Strangely enough it is individuals with the strongest sense of ego who claim they can accept the prospect of personal annihilation cheerfully. Unable to admit they might be in the hands of any higher authority they prefer to assume that when their life ends that is that. But though it seems to spring from a mature and unflinching acceptance of the true realities of life and death, this belief is remarkably similar to the young child's conviction that he is the centre of the universe and everything revolves around him. It is in the end all a matter of personal faith.

One of the most common beliefs to have persisted throughout human history is that funeral rites must be observed in order to free the soul and allow it to pass peacefully. Many people would be extremely distressed if they thought they would not be 'decently' buried and whatever else they sacrifice, they go to great lengths to put by the fairly substantial amounts of cash necessary for a big funeral with all the trimmings. Others leave detailed instructions about their disposal in their wills and need to be reassured that everything will be carried out according to their exact specifications.

The emotions personally connected with the prospect of their passing are what dictate the rites different people feel are necessary. In the cases of Kate's button phobia and Rowena's skin rash one might reasonably suppose that the distressing circumstances of their past deaths still linger and might be the cause of their distressing physical symptoms in the present. Many spirits desperately need to feel they have been shriven, pardoned or blessed before their departure from this world. Often there is a sense that it is not possible to pass over without appropriate assistance and some individuals seem to be acutely concerned even in their spiritual state if they think they have not received it.

Typically the necessary assistance does involve properly burying or praying over the departed but some individuals are particularly dependent members of human society and seem to need instead the reassurance that in spite of having lived possibly obscure lives, their fellow beings have granted them their entitled 'fifteen minutes of fame' after death. A full turnout by crowds, the bigger the better, is far more meaningful to them than any spiritual pardon or blessing.

There is no one rule or law about this and the reaction is based on what the spirits believed in this life, whether they were aware of it or not. They may have been carrying their beliefs from previous lives and been reluctant to acknowledge these even to themselves. Psychic work reveals many people are actually far more spiritual than they seem and can hold very deeply hidden convictions even they may not be aware of until they are placed in some situation that brings them to the surface.

Spirit or spirituality is generally perceived as weak and 'not real' in the modern world. Acceptance and the humbling of self appears to achieve much less than ambition, say, or other forms of 'positivity' popularly approved as mental disciplines that will complement material strength. We should never make assumptions based on the way an individual lives his life for it is not until he stands at the gate of death that his spirit will own its real needs and recognise how strong they are.

Sometimes the spirit has already departed before it knows itself what its own needs are. There was one case I had to deal with where a young man appeared to have lived a distinctly irregular kind of life involving drugs and sexual excess and a complete disregard for any spiritual belief. He committed suicide and his spirit made contact in great distress. It became apparent that he actually had a real need for the community values, the accepted customs of the 'old-fashioned' and formally 'religious' kind he had so completely rejected when he was alive.

His spirit wanted all the traditional trappings of death, to be properly buried with prayers and floral tributes, his death marked and remembered with pilgrimages made to some recognised resting-place or grave. It did not believe it could pass without them.

Many ghosts are supposed to haunt because their spirits are 'not resting' or 'not at peace'. I had never taken this claim seriously because I did not think it would matter to me where I was 'laid to rest' after death or even if I was laid to rest in the traditional manner at all. I found it difficult to understand other people's preoccupation with the details of funeral arrangements and insistence on elaborate headstones and grave plots kept unfailingly polished and neat, inclined to consider any distress if such rituals were not carried out to the letter as rather sad cases of over-reaction.

This was in my days of ignorance before I encountered cases like the ones I have just mentioned. Later I began to appreciate that every individual has a right to be just that, to have unique needs and to react in his or her own way if those needs are not met. The young man with his need for a recognised resting-place helped me to reassess my thoughts on the trappings and rituals of death. The place where their bodies have been laid acts for many spirits as a sort of launching pad into eternity without which they may well, as ghostly tradition insists, find it difficult to pass from the physical world.

Another case revealed how subtle the ramifications can be. One lady complained for years that she did not like the house where she had spent most of her married life and wanted to move to somewhere else. But when at last she died her spirit remained, refusing to leave. It was difficult to understand why and I worked with her spirit for some time until at last, detail by detail, explanations and answers emerged.

Though her greatest dream was supposedly to leave the house, she had believed she would never do so 'until I am carried out feet first in a wooden box'. In the event she suffered a bad fall, actually passing away in hospital but because she had not made her final exit from the house in the exact manner she had always anticipated she did not consider she had actually left it. I thought some sort of ritual handing over of the household power was called for since her extremely strong-willed and dominant personality had to be made to accept that her two sons were now in charge.

I suggested that her sons—now mature men but no doubt still immature boys in their mother's mind—should actually formally escort her spirit from the house. They could not take her out 'feet first in a wooden box' but they could perform a solemn ceremony, passing out through the front door in the way their mother had expected to go, bidding her goodbye and reassuring her that she could safely leave everything in their hands. She needed to be told firmly that she had to leave but her sons were the ones to conduct this leave-taking not a stranger.

The two men had never had any experience of sympathetic magic and I did not know whether they would feel able to carry out my instructions. Often I have recommended similar rituals to sitters who have found it difficult to let go of loved ones. Even if the deceased has been long buried or cremated and there is no grave to go to, formally lighting a candle and laying flowers or scattering them on running water and saying a prayer as the final goodbye is made can be helpful. To many these suggestions come as a wonderful revelation, giving them a way of mentally and spiritually taking control though there are those who inevitably react against what they see as spooky mumbo-jumbo with suspicion, even distaste.

I was told later by one of the two brothers that he, at least, had carried out the ritual, mentally taking his mother's hand in a personal gesture of faith and lovingly but firmly leading her from the house before saying his final goodbye and seeing her on her way. He now felt satisfied that the parting had at last been made and her spirit was no longer earth-bound.

Sometimes it can be the mourners who will not let the departed go. Violent grief and a refusal to try to accept that death has occurred can hold a spirit to the earth in spite of the fact that it might be ready and willing to depart.

I have been badly affected by problems of past death myself and realise this is the subject of the lesson I need to learn during my lifetime— or of one of them, for there are many lessons to learn, more than one task to address. Enlightenment is not quite so simple as we might like to believe. For instance though Rowena's skin rash did clear up after her Reiki session, it had returned when she came to see me a year later. We do not learn our lessons overnight. They continue through many lives and deaths as the spirit continues to develop in maturity.

It goes far deeper than just being able to die, learning to accept death. Acceptance and a willingness to submit to Spirit do allow us to achieve the same serenity of mind with which the animal kingdom can exist fully and joyously in the moment. Without any 'ego' standing in the way we can stop peering anxiously in all directions, continually apprehensive, nurturing and justifying our increasing fear.

But we have to be willing to offer some sort of payment, make some kind of sacrifice in thankfulness for what we have been given in life. It will be even better if we are not required to make any payment, if no high price is exacted from us but we need to be ready just in case there is, to take and accept whatever we must without flinching. When the spirit has progressed as far as this a great wonder occurs. The very willingness to accept the actuality of possible pain in life, possible suffering as we pass through the gates of death, reverses the debt. This does not mean that we will never suffer but that because we do not fear it, suffering no longer has the power to damage us.

I can recall a moment in a past life when I was a young fair-haired child (I think a boy) walking between two long rows of figures holding flaming torches. I had been chosen and was going to my death. This particular death experienced in some far corner of space and time, the agony of being disembowelled and torn apart while I lived has haunted me ever since. I could not accept nor free myself of that pain nor of what my own kind had done to me and why any gods there might have been had allowed it to happen. This is something felt within my being rather than thought through with my brain. But it has such a powerful hold that it has taken the repeated reassurances of Mist as I have worked at my spiritual development over the years to relieve the stifling terror enough to convince me I need not fear that old suffering any more.

'It is all over, the torchlit procession is over. It cannot hurt you now. It is finished.'

Our journeys have been repeated many times through many lifetimes in a kind of refining, educating process. Whether we are afraid is never the problem, what matters is how we face and deal with our fear.

We would all like to believe we have important business to carry out in our lives, some historic mark to make. But our real task does not involve living at all. We have to learn about dying. Many of us (myself included) need to learn how to tackle that final fence after so many bungled, inadequate attempts, approaching without fear so that we can make it this time and 'die successfully', having no need to come back to try again.

Norse mythology recounts how the dead hero

Donner was provided with a path to take him from this world to Valhalla across a wonderful rainbow bridge. In Wagner's *Das Rheingold* the composer actually creates the effect of the unfolding of the rainbow in rippling, luminously beautiful music. And perhaps this is how we too should view the death that lies before us—not as some grim, cold, painful trial we have to endure but as a rainbow bridge across which we can tread with wonder and delight.

I was describing a panic attack when I had feared I was going to die. 'Did you get that feeling of OOH, HERE WE GO?' asked my friend Geraldine, an astrologer and psychic medium. 'No, not really.' 'Then you weren't really dying.'

Chapter 7

The Silver Cord

Or ever the silver cord be loosed, or the golden bowl be broken, or the pitcher be broken at the fountain, or the wheel broken at the cistern.
Then shall the dust return to the earth as it was: and the spirit shall return to God who gave it.

The Book of Ecclesiastes

Sometimes people struggling to sort out their problems say to me rather sourly that 'It's all right for you. You're strong, you're liberated, you're self-contained.' Whether this is true is irrelevant, but if this is what they perceive when they look at me or talk to me they may well find it difficult to believe I could ever have been in their position.

Other people's problems always seem far easier to solve. And one of the sad truths you learn on your own journey through life is that you cannot pass on whatever wisdom you might acquire to anybody else. They will remain convinced their own journey is unique and cannot possibly be understood by others— and of course they are right. Each individual's

160

passage from birth to death is one he has to make single-handedly, a solo voyage in a frail craft battling its way through an uncharted ocean. The traveller must face and cope alone with whatever hazards he might encounter.

Sometimes, though, it can help to read accounts of the journeys other travellers have made across those lonely expanses of dark water, of the thoughts that were in their minds during their ordeals and how things seemed to them. This can hopefully prove inspirational, the next best thing to having actually been through the experience yourself.

I once undertook a forty-two day 'inner retreat' in the hope that I would find the advice and guidance I needed at that time. I was living alone in a one-room studio flat in London, just about to begin work on my third psychic book, *Celtic Wise Woman: The Secrets Revealed*, trying to escape from a relationship that had gone terribly wrong and to find the courage to go forward alone in whatever direction the spirits wanted me to go.

I questioned my own psychic ability, trying to let go my ego and cleanse myself of selfishness and negative attitudes and emotions in order to be a purer channel for the spiritual work I did every day. A friend had given me a Reiki healing session for my back pain and other

161

health problems and I had found it so 'mind-blowing' I wanted to study Reiki myself and become a Reiki healer—but, I wondered, was this a true vocation or some kind of ego-trip, seeking power?

For forty-two days I followed a course of intensive meditation, prayer and contemplation where I examined my self, my values and realities. I tried to listen to Spirit and express my willingness to be and do what was meant rather than what my ego might be putting in the way. Thirty minutes every day—without fail—was spent silently concentrating on various aspects of past and present experience, relationships, attitudes and feelings. What emerged then had to be worked on throughout the rest of the day and applied stringently to all my everyday living.

I have always loved the idea of making a formal 'retreat', perhaps staying in some beautiful monastery or abbey where the sound of bells and the simple beauties of nature would be calming and inspiring and the atmosphere of holiness would lift my soul. Yet it is not necessary to remove yourself from ordinary everyday reality—travel to the remotest heights of Tibet or shut yourself away in some room where no jarring note from the 'real world' is allowed to penetrate—in order to make your inner voyage of discovery.

It is against the background of the trials and tribulations of the 'world without' that the disciplines involved in taking a few moments each day to focus on the world within are most effective. How much easier to achieve spirituality and goodness when there is nothing except an atmosphere of spirituality and goodness around you—how much more vital and vibrant if you achieve and carry your own peace through the chaos and turmoil of an uncaringly material existence.

At the time of my 'retreat', I very much wanted to make a physical pilgrimage to Ireland, where I had unexpectedly experienced a great spiritual upliftment on a previous visit. I longed to return and the problem was not so much finance (for once!) as the fact that my health problems were so limiting. Apart from chronic pain and difficulty of movement, I was plagued by panic attacks at the prospect of travelling alone and thought I might quite literally die on the way—or at least, never manage to make the return journey.

I was fiercely determined though, to 'die living' if I was going to die at all just then. But again I wondered whether the idea of travelling to a beautiful country I loved expressed a real need or was just some selfish 'want' of my own.

During the forty-two days of my 'retreat' I kept the following notes. I wrote them more as expressions of my sensations and feelings of 'being' rather than with my head, as 'literature.'

I found I was getting into the habit of using short phrases like 'Blessings', 'Love' and 'Joy' as prayers, celebrations, invocations and in all the ways in which true magic works, by positively visualising and creating harmony in the midst of chaos.

During the course of the 'retreat' I existed on many planes of awareness. Apart from reaffirming my links with Spirit and with the spiritual beings who gave me guidance and wisdom to help me through my daily existence—particularly Mist, of course—I was granted a 'past life' recollection of another time and place where I had been and known my true self, reassuring and reaffirming.

I remembered a moment of great joy, an instant when I had lived as a true 'Celtic wise woman'—perhaps even recognised in the community and revered by her people—at some place in the middle of 1st or 2nd Century Britain during the time of the Roman occupation. I was standing in deep snow beside an expanse of water, with trees all around. Everything was covered with snow but the sky was tender blue, the sun was out, the winter day charged with gold. I was warm in a thick fur cloak, exhilarated and laughing. Ahead of me, across the icy black water of the lake a dark dot moved, leaving ripples arrowing in straight lines behind it—I knew it for the head of an otter.

The Retreat

Day 1
I felt as though it was all already done, that there was no problem. No fear, no pain. That I had been given the power that would push me forward. So thankful, there was nothing but thanks, balance, harmony.

Some difficulty over money since I have none and have to find £300 this week. I feel the spirits will cope but several weeks of being down to nothing with which to pay off debts have been eroding my confidence. It isn't the money so much, but the sense of restriction and lack of choice or freedom.

I felt a great sense of liberation afterwards.

I will take the step of courage and say—even so far as the money is concerned—

I *am* everything else I want, freedom and steadiness. Even the money. I will leave it and not worry.

It is done.

Day 2

I concentrated on all the good times I can remember in the past. This was very revealing in that I have had so many good experiences and good feelings, but they seem a long way off, as though they happened to somebody else. The memories seem as though I have run through them in my mind so often they are stale and tired, as though I have worn them out.

The one that touched me most was of a group session a couple of years ago where we all danced to someone drumming. One of the women was wearing only body paint which I found a bit startling since I was not accustomed to that sort of thing. She was so open and giving in the most lovely childlike way, truly trusting and sharing with everyone else and just shining with love.

She seems like an example I would like to copy (the love not the body-paint!) But even though I want to reawaken delight and spontaneity I

166

seem to have been completely cut off for a long time. Very difficult, a lot of work needed even to want these things at all, they do not seem to make much sense any more.

Very tired, feel tested and as though I have gone a long way alone. I cannot even remember what sweetness and innocence was like nor delight.

Black threads or if I was going back through water, it was fouled. I need to work here. Maybe this is what my sickness really is?

Thank you.

Day 3

Very much of a remembrance of growing and opening in power to theatre, plays, writing, acting and writing my books. I had no real sense that this was possible if I had lived an 'ordinary' life so I did a lot of manipulating people and situations in a desperate attempt to stay in control.

Perhaps I thought I could not achieve wisdom by staying 'ordinary'. Never felt as if I managed to be powerful or wise—as though I was condemned to be in some way restricted. But I metamorphosed during my twenties— definitely during my thirties—. Do I really want to be truly in control? Trying to want it, but seems difficult. Will try to accept it and do nothing just wait and see—I have to be pretty static anyway—but maybe it is not acceptance I have been doing but turning away and actually rejecting real control.

A big tiredness again. Need to work on it.

Thank you.

Day 4

I had to concentrate on my recollections of unconditional love. Seems further away than ever, I can't even recall whether I have ever experienced it at all. Seems like life and even all this is some sort of joke that I don't know about—even my own love has gone and I have none left. I realise this is just an illusion but it does not help my self-confidence and self-love. I do not feel any love anywhere or see any evidence of it. I feel difficulty in even believing. I seem to be going backwards not forwards.

Can I love my anger and pain? I'll try.

Wish I could say *it is done*.

Thank you. Thank you.

Day 5

A bit happier, I feel and see I am at rest in rays of moonlight, I am at peace here. But I wish there need be no words, they hinder communication.

Also aware of long-drawn-out difficulties in communicating with R., of desperation and saying nothing. I must learn to be silent— perhaps remember to keep silent hours during the day. I can do Buddhist meditation. The time has been so wonderfully given to me. (And my new book.)

Thank you. Thank you.

Day 6

I seem to have difficulty in being aware of the part of me that is the channel. It is difficult even to hold onto what I want to know when I open up to higher level.

I think I have lost all touch with my own position and need to know where I am so that I can start to ask for enlightenment. Almost like I have rubbed myself out.

I had a message about Ireland—very important, very strong.

I must go and leave all this chaos and confusion and constant doubt, feeling every word a joke and as though I have lost my sense of self—even that what I am trying to do in these meditations matters.

I'll find the answer, in however humble a way, somewhere else.

Thank you.

Day 7
Help me to hold onto my self and the light. Pride and fear do not matter—help me to let them go.

Thank you for showing me that I am tired and need a break, that it is not me/you at fault. Only weakness. Thank you for showing me possibilities I have forgotten.

Thank you my dear Mist, my guide and teacher. Be near me.

Love. Light.

Day 8

Thanks once more, so much thanks.

I was given the £300!!! (exactly!) today. Thank you.

Feel restrictions lift, I am able to see wide horizons, great sweeping vistas, anything will happen.

It would be good to find some new partnership—not like my recent disastrous marriage but a joining of trust, respect, rest and comfort. Quiet, no outrageousness. I doubt if the spirits will do that in a week!

Greenness, a wide land. A resting not restless passion. It would be lovely to be an equal, respected and cared for both as myself and as part of the other.

Maybe Ireland? But not for the blarney this time.

I feel anything is possible, fame, to laugh and be happy and content. A future.

Thank you my dear one.

Light. Love.

It Is Done.

171

Day 9

Much better today. I can see possibilities, a green Celtic land (Ireland?) I saw myself laughing, the image of myself as middle-aged, overweight Mum, drab and grey/brown dissolving into the lovely dignity and richness of myself in a long dress and cloak, upright and respected, bowed to for her worthiness, her birthright.

Started weight reduction programme today!

Having just quarrelled with R. I can see I am afraid to express my feelings either 1. In case I alter the status quo or 2. Because the other person may not be happy and I feel guilty at being happier, more famous, etc, than others. I stay on their level out of 'sympathy' and cannot see myself as separate with my own rights and feelings.

I must work on it—perhaps the real Celtic Wise Woman, the Lady Vivien or Morgan le Fay, will help.

Thank you.

I feel I may grow young again.

Day 10

Today I will accept the power and wisdom, it brings its own way of dealing with smaller things. I can take the power and wisdom of the Celtic Wise Woman from my vision of the winter lake, the inevitability of it all.

I had a jolting up today into 'manic' mode but was able to use it wisely and slow down. I am content to have the solitary weekend that lies ahead. I am concerned about the health problems R. has been complaining about but all senses tell me to draw aside and say nothing. He will not accept advice or help and only he can carry his own burdens, I cannot do it for him.

I am trying to think of happiness, strength, the green place, water, power. Power is not there so that you can put plasters on other people's mental scratches. R.'s fate is not in my hands.

Have only eaten very moderately today, feel I am being taken care of.

Thank you for the richness and the peace, for granting me a glimpse. I will be happy. I will be very famous.

It Is Done.

Day 11

I can see that I criticise out of need, but my needs are petty. When I get love and approval I react by freezing it out and criticising it. If I could see that others have to give me love in their own way I would be able to take the wonderful gift and not refuse it.

Day 12

Again I can feel the flow of silver passing through me, beyond words, like wisdom or telepathy I suppose. A balance between body and presence, truth and communication. I have rather a desperate feeling that I was always like this once and then I had to put a mask on—a silly, foolish mask—like trying to talk to unknown savages, knowing they would not understand me.

Silence is better.

I had forgotten the silent hours and Buddhist meditation. Breathe before I speak, I am too impulsive. Think of words not as casual but only there for emergencies.

I will speak only smiles and silence.

Communication is so precious.

Thank you. Thank you.

174

Day 13

A feeling of newness, as though I was a beginner, uncertain and not very good. I think I can sense the channel though it is difficult to understand the knowledge.

I don't think I realise the extent of the power. I wish for it but cannot even see what it is or how I can relate to it.

Please my dear ones, open my eyes and allow me to see the knowledge, to have ability not to do impressive things but to have the inner consciousness just to shine and be.

I don't think I feel worthy. Show me that I am.

Love. Light. Thank you.

Day 14

Difficulty in seeing the self at all. I have had a long, difficult day. The physical pull of the body and its restrictions and pain keep me down, also I feel restrictions when the shining energy disappears. I am very conscious of a sense of falling, as though I am failing in my duty—in conversation or trying to do the right thing all the time—so my human weaknesses turn to failings. I will try to shine and be, even when it's a very thin shining and being. The light will return—it is always there I suppose, but I feel my lack of energy and faith is something lacking in me.

Dear Mist—my Celtic Wise Woman and other selves—please be with me. This should not be a duty and a failing and criticism, I am sure.

Help me to shine for all of us.

Help me to be for all of us.

Love. Light. Trust.

Day 15

Today a calm sense that it will all happen and yet it is not necessary for it to happen. Things seem to be evening out so that everything is there and yet nothing. I wanted the fame, wealth, happy companionship and friendship and peace of mind—I will have it if it comes, if not it is no matter. I feel even more in the hands of the Self (or whatever) as though I am floating in a sea and land is not necessary.

Thank you for making me myself—I am proud of that, I share it with my True Self. This is all that really matters. The way, the trust to follow it and the energy that is ME.

I will have all I need with no effort or struggling.

It Is Done.

Love, my dear selves and Higher Self. Welcome dear Mist, be near me.

Day 16
Things have changed a lot. I have lost 2 lbs in one week!!

I can see that the feeling and acceptance stays with one into everyday, the letting go and then being able to know that the 'let go' person is accepted as she is, moving into 'non-feeling' or 'non-sensual' life.

The trouble is not in me, it is in others. I can do it all now, I have everything I ever wanted. Age is nothing. It does not matter, the letting go frees me.

But I must continue to work although the silver spring has started to bubble up again.

Thank you for allowing me to see the gold, but my dear Mist, you are silver.

Thank you. Love. Light.

Day 17

Oh how blind I have been because I never realised they were there all the time, the wisdom and the power. Behind the awareness in fear and upset, everything all there just the same, even my Celtic Wise Woman and my dear Mist who has seemed so far off lately.

I was afraid today of my eye test at the hospital. But I can see beyond, everything else is there too, my visions of the silver doves and the silver sea and probably more. The other life, the source, is there and never changes, I just need to accept in devotion and submission to it. I cannot cope, but my True Self can. That is such a wonderful thought, difficult to keep a hold on in these moments of fear and pain and panic. I need to learn to truly accept everything.

Thank you for my wonderful sense of being, I want to slip away into it and just SHINE, BE. Help me my dear Mist and give me the strength to take the power and the wisdom, to realise it is not me who needs to be in control.

Love and much light. Shining and being.

Day 18

It is fear that gets in the way, it happens when love becomes focused and visible. I think love has to be very quiet, very calm. Maybe love is just as simple as letting go of fear. The love just shines, it doesn't do anything. It just opens the way.

If the way is open, seems odd, difficult—not even giving anything, or taking, just being. It feels strange and as though nothing is there. Love is supposed to be a big thing, but it isn't. It is just the presence of no fear—in a weird way feels empty.

Love isn't sentimental. Nor emotional.

I have a lot to learn.

Dear Mist, let me see you are still there, even though the channel is empty.

Day 19

So many different sorts of communication. It is better without reactions, like just being there and sharing the being—but I don't know if this can happen on the physical plane. Can there be two awarenesses??

So often the communication problems are unasked for conversations, people you want to *not* communicate with. Words, speech is like rocks falling, then you fall over them. I feel no problem communicating the silver, it flows and is beautiful, but with the rocks—how does one deal with them?

Thank you for my books, for the learning I was given to try and 'express the silver'. I hope I can do this. Also thank you for the wisdom for chapters 1 and 2, given while I was meditating.

I am part of all of you, open to the truth and the silver, just being.

Thank you for being me.

Day 20

Today the channel seems to be stumbling on but not getting far. I feel my ignorance very much but I seem to want to have no self, no ego to make decisions. I thought about when I was a child, the things I did all the time without knowing why, and there is a sort of bewilderment now—I still don't seem to know.

I often feel myself make decisions and then not want to carry them out. But that is nothing to do with wisdom, the channel and true knowing. I feel I have lost my way today, but I won't give up—I caught a glimpse of the silver, the blue and everything.

You can't hold the vision, and probably I am trying too hard. The letting it go is more difficult. Do I have negative feelings like fear (my eyesight) and loneliness (tomorrow)??

Mist and my dear selves, be near and help me. I feel very vulnerable. Love. Thank you.

Day 21

Today I felt lumpy and stupid, difficulty even in reaching higher things, but I saw all the planes, every self a bit there. Perhaps the lack of coherence for myself—no wanting or feeling—is what I am aiming to put right. Very simple and unsensational, very quiet too, and not extreme. I feel it must be there, but just—there. No fireworks, all working together.

Thank you my dear Mist—and for what I have been feeling given to help my pain, as though hands are working on it all the time and the silver energy. Thank you my dear ones for being part of me. All of me. Love. Light. Blessings.

Day 22

It is done. I have been speaking to Aimi—I will be doing Reiki in October!

Everything will be taken care of, it is all going as it should.

Thank you. Love and light. Blessings on all of us.

Day 23
So strong. The Light, the Spirit, the Power, just there. I do not need to feel or think, just turn to it and SHINE. BE.

So the Light shines always and I reflect it in my own way. The strength is there unmoving and I feel it and lean on it.

IT IS DONE.

Love, light, blessings.

Thank you my dear ones for the calm and peace.

Day 24
Difficult to let go completely though I want to. I have no real desires. A house, rooms? Am I intended to live in one room?

I am grateful for this flat, I might have nothing. It is abundance, luxury.

I have so much.

Love. Light. Gratitude.

182

Blessings. Thank you.

Day 25
Shine. Be. The being is all.

I stand at the lake edge in winter snow, as I stood in a distant past when I was wise and knew all. I am laughing aloud with the joy. The dark head of an otter cuts like a spear through the black water.

I am.

My dear ones, thank you. Blessings.

Share the being.

Day 26
I have been under the impression that the vision/experience of unity with the Absolute happened then—and it was ten years ago. But now it is the same. There is no time. I have known then that *I am, to Shine and be*—and I still know it and I am confusing the issues by thinking times are different. They are the same.

I am the one who listens and speaks, achieves the silence and the quiet place. For myself. I will get no praise from thinking about or describing my struggles. They are irrelevant. Only to know that *I am* matters and that has always been there.

Thank you my silent other ones.

Blessings. Trust. Love. Light.

Day 27

I am getting a glimpse of the peace—but I think there is still some fear, uncertainty maybe when I am alone. But I am getting my space cleared and letting go. The past is gone—and yet not gone—but I don't need physical reminders. Now—the many nows—are what matters.

No need of results. Take and let go. The Light will provide.

I am surrounded by creatures of light and love.

I am freed from age, pain, lack.

Thank you, my dear ones.

Beauty. Love. Light. Joy.

Blessings—share the starry mist.

Day 28

Very tired but it is all very wonderful and amazing to think I was being guided on the way ten years ago. Have I progressed? I hope so, but as the card Aimi sent me says, 'You walk, You fall down, You get up—And all the time you keep on dancing'.

Thank you for friends, for leading me to Reiki, for letting me see that I do not have to put myself down any more—it is my right to BE myself fully, the same as it is for everyone.

It is a struggle but so worth it.

Thank you my dear ones for giving me the energy and for letting me come so far. In gratitude. Being. Shining. All of us.

Blessings. Thanks.

Light. (Love comes without having to be identified.)

Day 29

Simply to hold, that is all that is needed. Spirit, Power, Light, is what I am, all I need to know or want to know. Nothing else matters. This is truly the Source, the whole, everything.

No-one at home now only Spirit, Light, Source, Self.

Part of all and each now, not from outside of me.

Light, life, love.

Share the blessings and the peace.

Day 30
Every day the Light/Power/Spirit becomes steadier. I can let go more. There is no sense of need, only wonder at my blessings.

Thank you, thank you for all I have been given.

I still find it hard to cope with R. but I will become more sure of the answer. Can one be detached and yet 'humane'? The balance is difficult.

Light, life, power.

Day 31
I can see that heartfelt desires are to create space and light around me, not so much to get to anywhere else. Cleanness and space—perhaps the travel to Ireland too is right. I

have felt for a long time the need to wipe out dirt and chaos.

Material things don't matter, this does.

Materially, I can book my trip to Ireland through Harrods!

Problems being eased. I can let the past go. It was another world.

Day 32
The Light, Power, Spirit strengthens all the time, even when seeming to be tested and weak.

Thank you for my vision of the winter lake.

Solid reality.

Light, shining and being.

Day 33
It is becoming more real, that silver calm and power, the Light. I want to be there and feel how only that matters, the self is so irrelevant. I am becoming separate, there are other 'people' but I am increasingly conscious that they too are part of what I am letting go. The

power, light, spirit is all that is real. It gives the way through, there is no need to do anything.

SHINE. BE. Love. Light. Peace.

Day 34

I concentrate on the anger I feel at R. and the anger I have felt towards other men in past relationships. What starts off as unconditional love turns to anger because the other person is simply being himself. Why is this?

I want to change them, obviously, and I become unbearably frustrated and angry because they do not change. But if they altered it would not do them or me any good.

I not only become angry at the predictability of their patterns of self, but ashamed. I want them to transcend themselves—but with me organising the transformation. I want to create them.

Only when I let go of my need to regard them as my possessions will anger stop. I don't always see this clearly. Sometimes I seem at their mercy—I try to get them at mine. It is a battle. I cannot just SHINE, BE yet.

Day 35

I can see great strength.

I feel taking and accepting is important to consider because there is always the feeling that it is difficult for me to take, even ask or expect another to give to me—especially money.

I have contracts for work I have done which I cannot get paid for (actually I have been trying to get paid for years), I am trying to leave things like the contracts with the Light. Just wait and see.

I have a long way to go.

Is money to be counted on, is anything mine by right? Money is still in the way. And yet I am beginning to see it does not matter. There is abundance in everything if I can only have faith and trust.

Help me, my dear ones. Give me a sense of worth because

I AM and it is the right of

I AM, dignity and knowledge of itself.

Thank you for the winter lake, the otter, snow shadows.

Laughter. Light, blessings, joy.

Day 36
Sometimes it is stodgy and difficult to return to Source, probably I need cleansing and sorting out with the Reiki.

I AM and through 'nothing, empty' is the way to the Light.

Things weigh down. Go with the force, it provides for all, avoid the things of others which pull me down.

The force does not stay, it moves all the time.

Thank you for this awareness and for showing me things do not matter, they can go.

We are, we are, we are, in light and trust, shining and being.

Hold.

Day 37
Apart from 'want' there is also 'do not want', which expresses lack—lack of space to allow the abundance. Life and way of life full—but of the wrong things.

190

When tempted to over-react, unhook negative feelings as well as too much emotion.

Do not allow negative feelings in the guise of 'love' to cling. Go out the gate into the light.

Be tough.

Day 38

There seem to be no desires now, not even Ireland or a new place to live or for R. to be here in the evenings. Nothing 'heart felt'.

Perhaps my writing and some of the joy I had lost has come back. I do not need to go anywhere as a celebrity—let go that 'identity'. Go only as the Celtic Wise Woman, my own spirit, no social position.

I do not seem to really want for anything, I have so much.

Blessings, light, power.

Day 39

No emotional responses. Only consider, and take what comes. Lack of reactive 'hooks' results in ability to 'unfold' peacefully and calmly.

This needs working on.

The peace grows silver and serene and straight.

Day 40
Not feeling too well or else this is some sort of resistance. I do feel nothing—it must be all part of the plan.

I seem to have lost touch a bit—but I am sure this is the way and I will wait until I am shown what they want me to see.

Day 41
Love does not mean 'loving' other people or 'not loving' them. Unconditional love is the peace of Mist, the Little Spirits, the winter lake, not needing to react.

A freedom and wonder.

All 'connections' hook and trap the 'I'.

Thank you for the peace and the glimpses I have had of what lies beyond.

Day 42

How much better to expect nothing from anything or anyone.

I hope I am progressing.

Thank you for all my blessings, all my gifts.

Love, light.

The Spiritual Quest

*Channelled counsel from Brother Gregory
12th Century Augustinian monk*

How are you to find that rainbow of delight which in itself is many parts and yet is one whole surpassing beauty? Behold the rainbow of which all dream and will turn their eyes from the plough and the uneaten loaf to rest on nothing, their sinews tense, waiting the coming.

The knight with lowered visor on his horse will stir the dust at the end of a long road, so that even the leaves start, willing the commencement of the greatest venture of all. Shining stars tumble among the tangles of forget-me-not, and even worse than loss, the phantom with grinning skull-teeth and icy laden arms twining, which does not forget, making *never* a toll of doom.

Oh taste, for how else can the soul tell whether it is death that is behind the visor or the image of the eyes that beckon in the water. How else can the soul know the touch of the hand which will guide and embrace it and hold it in softest peace, unless it has first been willing to give itself to the stony talons that will rip it apart, for the sake of love.

I tell you, you must brave the storm and the fire and the three-fold death, the annihilation of your self for the sake of that other self which, parted from you and watching over you with yearning as you stumble the stones in your blindness, cannot be complete until you have earned for yourself the right to look up and see the face which is, in its alienation, yet your own. You will carry your sword fearfully, heavy in your arms, for the sake of the only one who can take it from you and gently lead you to your place beside the fire, and the protection of heaven.

What is human love compared? It is a flower that withers in a day, heedless, the petals fallen the next morning underfoot. I tell you the power of the life energy in every petal is a hundred thousand soft words and promises that will be broken. The human body cannot love, it can only perform as an organism to multiply. That which you call love is a linking to the light, the life, the silver power that reflects every leaf and petal in a different dimension so that the whole universe is transformed.

Have faith, dear child, that this word, this smile, will open not the gate of disillusion and poison at the bottom of the cup but the silver kingdom in which you belong.

A flight of doves in a courtyard, eternally rising into the face of the silver sun and lifting you, hands flying upwards with them, everything lightness, weightless.

Chapter 8

A Small Voice

'For most people the Grail was simply the golden core of whatever you dreamed you might achieve'
Phil Rickman *The Chalice*

'I think a hero is an ordinary individual who finds the strength to persevere and endure in spite of overwhelming obstacles'
Christopher Reeve *Still Me*

The whole point about heroes is that they are not ordinary. Yet as we have already discussed, they are not extra-ordinary either. The heroic potential is there within all of us, a 'golden core' that (though we might not really believe in it ourselves) shines out as a light to draw others on through the murk of the everyday world and inspire them too to attempt higher and better things. And the most enduring symbol of the heroic is perhaps the story of King Arthur and his knights, the story of 'many-towered Camelot' and its visionary monarch who fired his followers to dedicate themselves to the greatest quest of all—the search for the Holy Grail.

I have always found it easy to identify personally with ancient worlds and ideals of chivalry and romance. Welsh-born into a Welsh-speaking family, my grandmother and grandfather on my mother's side (my 'Nain' and 'Taid') generally speaking only Welsh, I accepted the tales from the *Mabinogion* and all the stories of Celtic folk myth as simply a part of my personal heritage. They became woven into my identity.

As a child I took this state of affairs for granted. Later as an aspiring writer I turned to my background for inspiration and had no hesitation in launching my freelance career by writing local history articles and town and county guide books that covered my home area of North Wales to saturation point. With whoever I could find in tow to take pictures, I explored almost every ancient ruin, castle, standing stone and healing spring or stream there was and read up on all the old stories and legends available in libraries.

I had tried to capture the essence of my Welsh heritage and what it meant to me in a script called *Welsh Tapestry* that I once wrote for BBC Radio Merseyside.

'What does it mean to you, that word "Wales"?' my Narrator asked briskly. 'Makes you think of witches' hats and red flannel?

Llanfair-whatsit and the Eisteddfod at Llangollen? Old ladies spinning in garish picture-postcard colours outside a stone farmhouse in the mountains?

'That may be all the word means when it is only a word. But when it is not just a word, what then?'

Ah, indeed what then? While I was writing the script there was an image of some kind of heroic figure at the back of my mind but it was not the image of an ancient prince, knight or nobleman. Actually, the figure I envisaged was that of my Welsh grandfather, my 'Taid', who had been a typical working man of the early 20th Century.

Taid had been born into the steel industry and I grew up in the shadow of steel myself, in a small village dominated by the Steel Works that loomed above it and dominated it. But Taid's family—my great-grandparents and their thirteen children—had actually occupied a large house in earlier years within the environs of the Works complex itself, at the side of 'the Line' where the trains with their wagons were constantly shunting to and fro. My great-grandfather had apparently held quite a responsible position in the offices and had travelled to Russia several times as a representative for the (then, I think) Brymbo

Steel Company. So added to my heritage of Welsh myth I could also claim some small connection with the richness of the Imperial Court of the Tsars, where one of my forebears had actually trodden the gilded and jewelled corridors and bowed before the Father of All the Russias.

Family tradition recounted how the traveller returned wearing an immense fur coat and Russian hat, and the women of the household refused to let him in until he—and his garments—had been 'fumigated' against whatever 'foreign' bugs they might be harbouring. But I never saw any actual evidence of those trips to Russia and whatever money the family might have had in its days of glory had long since been lost by the time my Taid, the youngest child, grew to manhood.

He started in the Works as a lad of thirteen and by the time of his eventual death in his sixties—just before he was to retire—he had risen to the position of Foreman in the Fitting Shop, an achievement of which he was very proud. He was known and deeply respected throughout the whole community and I grew up, as it were, in his shadow, under the protection of his name. My own name and identity counted for little but as 'Gwilym Ivor's grand-daughter' I was accepted and welcomed without question everywhere.

I remember Taid as a 'gentle giant'. A big man (at least, he seemed big to his grand-daughter) and of few words. To me he always seemed very much a distant patriarchal figure and I never felt I could get cosily close to him, he was not that sort of a person. Sometimes too, he could speak very brusquely.

I never saw Taid read a book and he rarely wrote letters. He was a physical person, a man of action not a thinker. Yet in the years after his death when I was researching for a novel about the First World War, I came across a small paper-bound volume that had belonged to Taid which he had kept since he had himself served in the 'Great War' as a young soldier. He had been in Salonika, where he contracted malaria. As a child I believed it was the malaria that had caused him to become almost bald at a young age. Whether this was true or not I don't know but Taid was very self-conscious about his shining pate and always wore a flat cap, with such dignity it might have been a helmet of office.

The small yellow-bound book he had kept among his few personal possessions was called *Rough Rhymes of a Padre* by 'Woodbine Willie' (G. A. Studdert-Kennedy, M.C., C.F.), who I discovered when I did my research had served as a chaplain with the British Expeditionary

Forces. He had written several small books of inspirational verse that had been very popular among the men and when I read *Rough Rhymes* it was easy to see why.

These had been poems any ordinary soldier in the ranks would have been able to relate to, any young lad like my Taid with little formal education and no interest in 'culture', thinking about his sweetheart back home and with all his life before him. Facing the prospect of perhaps being blinded, maimed or killed in some of the most brutal and gruesome fighting the world had ever seen, he would have been able to clutch and hold onto 'Woodbine Willie's' words, written in language he could appreciate and understand, in the dark hours before the dawn.

In my novel about the First World War —*A Man of Honour*—my hero Major Hilary Dunton, wounded and back from the Front, also possessed a copy of one of 'Woodbine Willie's' poems that had kept him sane and steady. (But because the verses had not at the date of my story been published in book form he had to carry his with him on a much-thumbed piece of folded paper.)

In my novel he asked his nurse to read them to him as he lay in his hospital bed, a little on the defensive because he was an officer who might have been expected to take inspiration from some deep philosophical treatise rather than a piece of rough doggerel.

When there ain't no gal to kiss you,
And the postman seems to miss you,
And the fags have skipped an issue,
                    Carry On

When you've got an empty belly,
And the bulley's rotten smelly,
And you're shivering like a jelly,
                    Carry On

I was a little surprised that my Taid—never, so far as I was aware, an overtly spiritual man—had had such a book in his possession. I was even more interested when I discovered an old scrap of paper that at some time he must have tucked casually into it, perhaps to mark a favourite page. On one side was a shopping list where items like '2oz Tea' and 'Small bag Flour' had been laboriously penned—or rather, pencilled—in faded script. On the other, just as randomly, were a few words that indicated Taid had been trying to explore the great mysteries of life in his own way. They made no real sense and seemed to come to no conclusion, but were simply his own jottings about 'The Soul—goes on?' and 'Spiritual Life??' and 'God??'.

It was this small piece of paper revealing the man I had never really known that was in my mind when I was writing my *Welsh Tapestry*. Heroes do not always come in shining armour, on a white horse with a sword in their hand.

In legend and myth as well as in real life, there must have been many men just like my Taid. There have always been the unsung battalions—inarticulate, unprivileged, dispensable cannon-fodder—whose presence and willingness to do what they are told has been what has won or lost battles and wars. The ordinary fighting man usually complained loudly about his lot but he got on with the job, though more focused on his creature comforts than any 'high ideals and noble resolves'. He might not have been a philosopher or a scholar but he too could feel fear at the prospect of what the forthcoming day of battle might hold. He too probably experienced the stirring of something he could not put into words within his soul as he sat waiting for the morning and looking at the stars. And it was of such men that I was thinking as I wrote in *Welsh Tapestry*:

> *The spirit of her people is like finest steel, not*
> *   to be bent, not to be broken*
> *Though many fires it has been tempered in.*
> *It remains yet, this sword of Wales,*

*Priceless in the hands of the poor as well as
    the rich.*

*Work-roughened fingers are on the hilt, and
    who does not straighten his weary back as
    royally as a king,
Unknowingly assuming his inheritance, the
    imperishable dignity*

*That is the birthright of all who wear the
    sword?
Proud in the scabbard lies the blade passed on
    by forgotten ancestors
Treasured by her people as a symbol of
    honourable vassalage to their liege.*

With my Celtic background I found it easy to think and express myself in the terms of heroic chivalry. But on my father's side my roots were deep in the realism and practicality of London's East End. My father—another man who had never appeared to be spiritually inclined—had actually written a 'send-up' of chivalric idealism when as a young aspiring writer he had composed his own irreverent version of Tennyson's *Excelsior!*

I had always responded ardently to Tennyson's Arthurian poetry, dimmed with rich colours and drenched in romance. When I read *Sir Galahad* I was so smitten by this stained-glass picture of a peerless knight that I kept a copy for years and used to quote it comfortingly to myself to counter the brashness and too-real physicality of the young men I met as a teenager. Sir Galahad was my hero:

My good blade carves the casques of men
My tough lance thrusteth sure
My strength is as the strength of ten
Because my heart is pure.

Tennyson's *Excelsior!* was a praiseworthy exhortation to strive ever 'Onwards and Upwards' but my Dad was a man with his own quirky sense of humour and his feet on the ground. The poet had written with hushed and solemn gravity:

The shades of night were falling fast
When through the Alpine village passed
A youth, who bore 'mid snow and ice
A banner with a strange device—
                    Excelsior!

The youth with his banner, his face turned nobly towards the high peaks of the mountains and visions of achievement, was meant to provide inspiration to everyone who heard his story as well as to the dwellers in that story-book Alpine village. But my Dad updated the tale, turning it into a horror-thriller and setting it against a more modern background:

206

The shades of night were falling fast
When through the cemetery passed
A youth who bore upon his back
A concrete tombstone in a sack!

Upon the breeze, a sigh, a moan,
Then a weird, unearthly groan.
He paused, and looked this way and that—
Surely he'd stepped upon the cat?—

My Dad too had been a soldier but in the World War that came after the mud and blood of Salonika and the Somme and Flanders, and perhaps in the doggerel verses he loved to compose there was another of those unknown heroes speaking. Dad was not spiritually inclined either but the use of irreverent humour when dealing with the great mysteries of life is just one of the weapons by means of which those who are aware of the immensities—and perhaps frightened by them—try to protect themselves.

I cannot say that I have always understood this. As a young girl I was a great sentimentalist. I did not care for the seeming harshness of reality and preferred to drown myself in passionate romance. Once I even wrote a long epic novel called *The Twisted Stems*, based on the love story of Tristram and Iseult as portrayed in the works of Sir Thomas Malory—the source from which Tennyson took his *Idylls of the King*. It was unfortunately never published (too much self-indulgence on my part, since Tristram had now taken the place of Sir Galahad as my romantic hero) but I did research Arthur and his times quite seriously for a non-fiction book on Welsh history called *The Battles of Wales.*

Welsh legend places Camelot at Caerleon-on-Usk and Welsh tradition claims that King Arthur and his knights have never left Wales. They are only sleeping (in a great cave deep in the heart of the mountains of Snowdonia, some say), held in a tranced slumber that will be broken when they are needed again. A horn will sound and they will rise and ride out in all their richness and flower of chivalric endeavour to fight for Wales.

Other versions of the Arthur story claim Camelot and Arthur's resting-place for themselves and set them in other places. They are, like the Grail, symbolic rather than factual. Whether Arthur and Camelot ever even existed does not matter. It is what they represent.

The search for the Grail is the search for ourselves, for what we might be if only we can be big enough—or even if we can only find that desire to strive for something within ourselves. It is not the finding of the Grail that matters but the wanting to search for it, the belief that somewhere there is a Grail.

In Christian tradition the Holy Grail was the cup from which Jesus drank at the Last Supper, imbued with grace. But it is not just a Christian image. Ancient Celtic tradition with its roots in the paganism of an era that flourished long before Christianity came to the west portrays a cup as one of the four Celtic 'Holy Treasures'. This image is of a cauldron sometimes presided over by the frightening Celtic goddess-crone Ceridwen, a dark cauldron that is the cauldron of plenty but also where all transformation takes place.

Since transformation is never accomplished without struggle and difficulty the cauldron of Ceridwen is the melting-pot of destiny—the same melting-pot perhaps where ordinary people can achieve something greater than themselves and reach heroic stature.

We can take whatever routes we like in this world but we will never ever be able to escape from ourselves, even if we do not know what those selves are. After I had been writing for nearly thirty years I looked back over the thirty-odd novels I had written and found that every one of them had had a central theme, however deeply it had been hidden. They had been accounts of the struggle for identity and though I had been expressing this struggle through my characters the striving for selfhood was of course basically my own.

At one stage I rebelled against my Welsh background. The years I had spent tramping the ancient monuments of North Wales in my research with notebook at the ready, sitting poring over ancient maps and documents and reference books in libraries, reconstructing tales and legends, suddenly seemed to pall. I no longer found the sound of spoken Welsh, the music of the harp and *penillion* singing, the love poetry of the early princes—which had fed my soul since I was young—meant anything to me. I did not, when I came to think about it, even care for my own name, which is an unusual Welsh one. I spent some time being ashamed of all that life had given me in its richness and fullness and wanting to disown it.

Perhaps we all do this as we mature. We have to rebel against the realities we are presented with, test them to see whether they prove themselves. We all have to set out on our own heroic Quest to find our own version of the Grail, to slay demons and dragons, meet the challenges and tests we are set in order to achieve our potential stature. Yet even as we undertake this Quest we have to also understand that in some way the very willingness to undertake it means that it has already been fulfilled.

One of the more subtle aspects of the Quest is that even the knights who set out on it did not know what they were really looking for. Parsifal, who found the Holy Grail, saw it in a vision but he did not recognise it or know what he was supposed to do about it. In just the same way it is the travelling rather than the arrival on which we should be concentrating as we journey through our lives. Once we have reached journey's end—wherever or whatever it proves to be—we will find ourselves in a whole new ball game (to use the modern idiom) and we will have to start all over again.

One of the tarot cards in the deck I use—the Prince of Cups—is illustrated with a picture of Parsifal holding the Holy Grail. But he is not looking at it. His eyes are still striving forward, seeking. He does not realise he has actually come to the end of his Quest and holds the Grail in his hands.

On the night before he set out on his Quest a knight would keep a vigil kneeling before the altar of a church, dedicating his sword and himself to God. In the morning he set out in faith into the unknown.

We can aim at our goals, focus our energies on what we hope to achieve—but the rest we have to place, as the knights did, in the hands of the higher power. We can travel hopefully and enjoy the journey. Since we do not know what the end is going to be we are simply wasting time if we try to anticipate it.

And whenever we find ourselves in difficulties on whichever of the many roads we happen to be travelling—even if we do not even know in which direction we are heading—we can ask for guidance. Not necessarily by holding a night of vigil, just a few moments quietly alone will enable us to reaffirm our sense of identity and reconnect with whatever higher power we trust to see us safely through.

Some call it praying. Some call it meditation. Whatever you call it, the effect is positive and uplifting and the answer we need is always there. But in all the clamour of modern life, the noise and advice and admonition, exhortation and command and blame, all the ways in which the physical world expresses itself so loudly, it is sometimes very difficult to hear the small voice of the spirit.

Whenever I have come to my own spiritual source in anxiety or distress seeking assistance and comfort, pleading to be told what to do, which way to go, how to find the answer, work out a problem, overcome an obstacle, I have always received exactly the same message. It has calmed me, soothed my fears and given me all the advice, wisdom and strength I will ever need to enable me to carry on. It is not about doing things, piling up book-learning, being successful. It is not street-wise, smart or clever. The voice of the spirit speaks very gently, very quietly. But it says everything in two short words of instruction:

Shine. Be.

We did not travel for adventures, nor for company,
but to see with our eyes, and to measure with our hearts
John Ruskin *Praeterita*

It is good to have an end to journey towards,
but it is the journey that matters in the end
Ursula Le Guin
The Left Hand of Darkness